/05

ω

REMINISCENCES OF
A SOLDIER'S WIFE

Very Sincerely Yours
Ellen M. G. Biddle

REMINISCENCES OF A SOLDIER'S WIFE

ELLEN McGOWAN BIDDLE

With a new introduction by Peter Cozzens

STACKPOLE
BOOKS

New introduction © 2002 by Stackpole Books

Published by
STACKPOLE BOOKS
5067 Ritter Road
Mechanicsburg, PA 17055
www.stackpolebooks.com

Cover design by Tracy Patterson
Cover photo (left to right): Act. Master John McGowan, U.S.N., Ellen
McGowan Biddle, and Col. James Biddle, 6th Reg. Indiana Volunteer
Cavalry. Courtesy of the U.S. Army Military History Institute.

Printed in the United States of America

10 9 8 7 6 5 4 3 2 1

FIRST EDITION

Library of Congress Cataloging-in-Publication Data

Biddle, Ellen McGowan, b. 1841.
    Reminiscences of a soldier's wife / Ellen McGowan Biddle ; with a
new introduction by Peter Cozzens.— 1st ed.
       p. ; cm. — (Frontier Classics)
    Originally published: Philadelphia : J.B. Lippincott, 1907.
    ISBN 0-8117-2058-6
    1. Biddle, Ellen McGowan, b. 1841. 2. Women pioneers—West
(U.S.)—Biography. 3. Army spouses—West (U.S.)—Biography. 4.
Pioneers—West (U.S.)— Biography. 5. Frontier and pioneer life—
West (U.S.) 6. United States. Army—Military life—History—19th
century. 7. West (U.S.)—Social life and customs—19th century.
8. West (U.S.)—Description and travel. 9. Southern States—
Description and travel. 10. West (U.S.)—Biography. I. Title.
II. Series.

F594 .B58 2002
978'.02'092—dc21   2002018816

TO MY CHILDREN

Who have brought me so much joy and happiness

INTRODUCTION

by Peter Cozzens

Life for an army officer's wife on the post–Civil War frontier was hard—incomprehensibly hard for young women accustomed to the comforts of proper society. Hailing for the most part from upper middle-class Eastern homes, army brides had only the vaguest notion—if they had any notion at all—of what awaited them at the primitive and distant posts to which their husbands were often assigned. Offering words of caution based on a decade of frontier duty, one army surgeon warned, "Let all young ladies who are dazzled with the glare of gilt buttons at some of the fashionable parties on East, bear these and other deprivations in mind before saying 'yes' to the fascinating Sons of Mars."

Few heeded such advice. Love, a sense of duty, and a few disingenuous words from the army high command carried officers' brides west. Speaking to a group of army wives in St. Louis just after the Civil War, Maj. Gen. William T. Sherman promised a "healthful and pleasant" life, free of deprivation or fears of Indian attack, for those who accompanied their husbands on their western assignments. Instead, remembered one young wife, what they found was a life of "glittering misery."

Be it from Indians, blizzards, locusts, illness, or overland travel, danger was ever present. Hardships were many and varied. No special allowances were paid to married officers, and no provision made for quartering their dependents. Officers without independent sources of income could seldom afford to keep their families at post for long.

Officially, the army did little to help. Officers' wives lacked even official status at post. Elaborate regulations governed the remuneration of laundresses and the conduct of prostitutes, or "camp followers," but officers' wives were official nonentities. Their mere presence in garrison depended on the whim of the commanding officer, who could order them away at his discretion. Should their husbands be killed in the line of duty, widows were expected to vacate the quarters of the deceased and leave post at once.

Not that army quarters were worth keeping. While quarters varied widely from post to post, most company-grade officers and their families had to make do with two or three small rooms. Furniture was often crude and homemade. Dirt floors and leaky roofs were common at small posts, and even the largest and best appointed garrison communities seldom had indoor plumbing. Housing hinged upon rank and seniority. Through an informal process known as "bricks falling," a newly arrived officer might appropriate for his own use the quarters of any subordinate officer, turning out the underling and his family without notice of eviction. The bricks fell particularly hard on one lieutenant and his bride at Fort Clark, Texas, who were ranked out of their single room and into a hallway.

In addition to poor housing, officers' wives at small or isolated posts often had to contend with poor food and chronic shortages of fruits and vegetables. Schooling also was a problem, and many families were compelled to send their older children East to boarding schools for a proper education. Domestic help was scarce and expensive; no sooner did a female servant or nurse reach post than she would quit to marry an enlisted man. The difficulties of childcare paled, however, beside the acute dangers accompanying childbirth itself. Poor sanitation and rudimentary medical attention caused many women to develop "childbed fever" or other serious postpartum complications. Miscarriages were common, and it was the rare family that did not lose at least one child at or shortly after birth.

Officers' wives had to contend not only with danger and discomfort, but also with drudgery. Diversions tended to be simple and few. Horseback riding, fishing, picnics, and target shooting helped pass the time. Dances, or "hops," were organized whenever there were enough women at post. Other popular distractions included amateur theatrics, dinner parties, and sewing bees. Less salutary to post morale was the tendency of wives to gossip and splinter into rank-based "affinity cliques." Not surprisingly, given their isolation from society, officers' wives tended to be poorly informed, and they often came across as shallow. One resentful enlisted man derided the officers' women of his regiment as "painted dolls." A bitter former officer remarked that wives and whiskey were the worst possible influences on an army post.

Yet there were exceptional women among the ranks of officers' wives, several of whom published reminiscences of their experiences. To their books, we owe much of our understanding of frontier army life. Perhaps the most famous of the genre is Elizabeth Bacon Custer's trilogy of life with the 7th U.S. Cavalry, *Tenting on the Plains, Following the*

Guidon, and *Boots and Saddles*. She wrote to perpetuate the memory of—and weave legends around— her late husband, George Armstrong Custer, which decidedly mars the value of her books. Generally more honest are the recollections of wives of less notable officers, most of whom wrote after their husbands had retired and simply for the benefit of friends and family.

Such was the case with Ellen McGowan Biddle, who penned her *Reminiscences of a Soldier's Wife* for her grandchildren in 1907, and whose publisher sold the book by subscription. Ironically, it was not her many years on the frontier that inspired Ellen to write, but rather a few short months spent in Mississippi during Reconstruction.

Ellen wrote from the heart. In the brief preface to *Reminiscences of a Soldier's Wife*, she said that it was while sitting on the rose-covered porch of her daughter's home in Santa Barbara, California, "with the odor of jasmine, heliotrope, and magnolia all about me, [that] my thoughts went back to the delightful days of my life spent in Mississippi, [and] the inspiration came upon me to write the reminiscences of my army life, beginning in that beloved state."

If not necessarily better prepared for army life than other young brides, Ellen McGowan Biddle at least had better cause to stick it out, having been raised in a military household. Her father, John McGowan, had entered the United States Navy in 1832 as a warrant officer aboard the cutter *Gallatin*. Twenty-eight years old when he began his naval service, the elder McGowan was still on duty at the outbreak of the Civil War. Although too old for extended service at sea, Captain McGowan achieved a fleeting fame early in the conflict. He happened to be on duty at New York harbor in December 1860, when Pres. Abraham Lincoln tried to victual the Federal garrison at Fort Sumter. Captain McGowan was assigned command of the steamer *Star of the West*, which made the effort on June 9, 1861. Secessionist batteries at the mouth of Charleston harbor blocked the attempt, and the *Star of the West* returned to New York. There McGowan remained, passing the war in relative comfort as commander of the U.S. revenue steamer *Cuyahoga*.

Captain McGowan's son (and Ellen's older brother), John McGowan, Jr., followed his father into the navy during the Civil War. As an acting master he saw duty first in the Potomac Flotilla, and later in the North Atlantic Blockading Squadron. The younger McGowan continued in the Regular service after the war, and by 1904 had risen to the rank of rear admiral. Ellen's brother-in-law, D. B. Harmony, was also a navy man. Official records show him in command of the U.S.S. gunboat *Tahoma* in the East Gulf Blockading Squadron in 1864 with the rank of lieutenant commander. Ellen also had a younger brother, who as a sixteen-year-old youth served in Gen. Ulysses S. Grant's army at Vicksburg in 1863.

Being the daughter of a navy, rather than an army, officer, Ellen McGowan had the advantage of growing up in comfortable and civilized surroundings. Raised in Elizabeth, New Jersey, a "quiet little church-going town," as she put it, Ellen "had been one of a large family and accustomed to a large home; though not so elegant, it was filled with gay laughter and joyful sounds." Her family were members of Saint John's Episcopal Church.

Ellen was born in 1847 and married at age seventeen. Her husband, James Biddle (born December 11, 1832), was fifteen years her senior and the scion of a distinguished Philadelphia family. James descended from William Biddle, a shoemaker by trade and a colonel in Cromwell's army during the English Civil War, who came to America in 1681 and purchased a large tract in western New Jersey from William Penn. William Biddle's grandson John moved to Philadelphia in 1730 and engaged in shipping and importing. There he married Sarah Owen, with whom he had six children.

The second child of John and Sarah was Clement Biddle (1740–1814), a Revolutionary War hero and close friend of George Washington. Clement Biddle played a prominent role in the battle of Trenton, where Washington accorded him the honor of receiving the swords of the surrendered Hessian officers, and he later served on the staff of Nathaniel Greene. After the Revolution he worked in the import business in Philadelphia and held both state and federal office.

Clement Biddle was James's grandfather. James's father was Edward Robert Biddle (born February 7, 1798), one of thirteen children of Clement and Rebekah Cornell Biddle. Rebekah was the daughter of the lieutenant governor of Rhode Island. Among James's other illustrious relatives was his great uncle, Nicholas Biddle (1786–1844), one of the foremost scholars, statesmen, and financiers of early America and a leading member of Philadelphia society.

James Biddle was a twice-brevetted, veteran volunteer officer when he married Ellen in late 1864. Biddle had entered the Union army in May 1861 as first lieutenant and quartermaster of the 10th New York Infantry, a ninety-day regiment that spent its brief federal service quietly at

Fortress Monroe, Virginia. Biddle re-entered the army in August as a captain in the newly organized 15th U.S. Infantry. Both Regular officers and civilians were accorded commissions in the regiment. Oliver L. Shepherd, a West Point graduate and Mexican War veteran, was appointed colonel. John P. Sanderson, a prominent Philadelphian, was named lieutenant colonel.

Although Sanderson may have helped Biddle obtain his appointment, the War Department set high standards for commissioning. General Orders No. 33 stated:

> The newly appointed officers will lose no time in making themselves thoroughly acquainted with the army regulations, the tactics of their several arms, and the various duties of their profession. None will be nominated for commissions to the Senate who have not proved themselves, meantime, to be both worthy and capable of commanding the brave men under them. That the Department may be enabled to form a proper judgment on this delicate point, all commanding officers will forward to this office a statement on honor of the moral, mental, and physical qualifications for the service of each one of the officers belonging to their command.

Four weeks after earning his commission, Biddle found himself in the theatre of war, on duty with the 15th Infantry in Kentucky. The regiment saw its first action at the battle of

Shiloh in April 1862. Five months later, Captain Biddle distinguished himself at the battle of Richmond, Kentucky. His presence in the battle was a matter of chance; Biddle happened to be in Richmond on detached duty as an army paymaster, paying members of the 71st Indiana Infantry their enlistment bounty, when the Confederates attacked the town. Biddle went into action with the 71st, taking command after the lieutenant colonel and major were killed. The brigade commander cited Biddle for gallantry and acknowledged his "particular obligations to Captain Biddle for valuable suggestions in relation to the posting and ranging of the artillery." For his service at Richmond, Biddle was brevetted a major in the Regular army.

When the 71st Indiana reorganized in November 1862 as cavalry, Gov. Charles P. Morton acceded to the request of its officers and men that Biddle be appointed colonel. Under Biddle's command, the 6th Indiana Cavalry fought in the Knoxville, Atlanta, and Nashville campaigns. Biddle was captured near Macon, Georgia, during the Atlanta campaign, and the story of his subsequent captivity and exchange—told in his own words—forms a humorous postscript to Ellen's *Reminiscences*. Biddle earned his second brevet, to lieutenant colonel in the Regular army, for gallantry at the battle of Nashville, where his troopers fought as dismounted infantry. Biddle had erred in permitting his men to wear their sabers while making an uphill charge, which caused them to stumble and trip over their scabbards, but his division commander forgave the colonel's "shortsightedness." Colonel Biddle concluded the war with one final brevet, to brigadier general of volunteers on March 13, 1865 for "long, gallant, and meritorious service."

Such was the Civil War record of James Biddle. For a picture of the man behind the brevets we are indebted to Ellen. The portrait of her husband that emerges in *Reminiscences of a Soldier's Wife* accords well with both the official record and the opinions of his fellow officers. Biddle was a large man, weighing some two hundred pounds, athletic and "tremendously strong," said Ellen. He drank little and possessed an openhanded geniality. His good nature and "adaptability" won him many Southern friends during Reconstruction duty in Georgia and Mississippi, and later in life earned him the devotion of the Black soldiers of the 9th U.S. Cavalry. The Biddles enjoyed entertaining and kept an open house during their entire military life. Her husband loved music, averred Ellen, but was at heart an outdoorsman. An avid hunter, Biddle took pride in being the top marksman in the Departments of the Missouri and Arizona.

Ellen's character we must reconstruct from her own words or from clues found in *Reminiscences of a Soldier's Wife*. She had lived a sheltered life before her marriage. "I had not gone into society before my marriage (being considered too young)," said Ellen, "and knew but little of the gay world, except what I had seen at my father's house." Although saddled with two small children, Ellen partook fully of Southern society during the couple's Reconstruction assignments in Macon, Georgia, and Natchez, Mississippi. Like her husband, Ellen found that she adapted readily to new surroundings. She came to love the opera and dancing, as well as the outdoor life of the South. Natchez "was delightful, and some of the warmest and dearest friends of my life were made [there]. We often went fox hunting, getting up in the early morning to be off before day." It was at Natchez that

Ellen "unfolded as the flowers did and developed from the girl into the woman."

That unfolding did not extend to her health. A recurring theme in *Reminiscences of a Soldier's Life* is Ellen's lifelong struggle with poor health. Ellen was so slender as to strike some as fragile. "I cannot understand how frail women like you and Ellen," Col. Joseph G. Crane, the Reconstruction mayor of Jackson, Mississippi, told a mutual lady friend in 1869, "who look as if a gentle wind would blow you over, can dance as you do; why, you seem to possess more endurance than a government mule."

Ellen's endurance was repeatedly tested during her army life. While traveling to Savannah from New York by sea in the summer of 1866 to join James at Macon, she suffered from sudden fainting spells. At Natchez in 1869 she contracted yellow fever. The disease badly weakened her already delicate constitution. "It took me a long while to recover from the effects of that disease, and I always thought I never looked quite the same after it. The freshness of youth was gone," lamented Ellen. Her fainting spells returned later that year, during their next—and least pleasant—assignment, in Texas. Frayed nerves and illness compelled her to return to her parents' home, and for several weeks she lay near death. Ellen fell desperately ill again in 1872, while the couple was posted at Fort Halleck, Nevada. She miscarried and was confined to bed for three months. Her poor health caused her next child to be born "frail and delicate," and it died three weeks after birth in June 1877.

In all, six children were born to Ellen and James Biddle, four of them on the frontier. John and David Harmony Biddle came respectively in 1866 and 1867, before Ellen left the

East Coast. Ellen McGowan Biddle, or "Nellie," as her parents called her, was born in 1869. James Harwood Biddle died in infancy in 1877. Nicholas Biddle was born in the winter of 1879. Alice Biddle was born the following year and died of illness in August 1885.

The accomplishments of the Biddle children who survived to adulthood demonstrate that Ellen McGowan Biddle was no ordinary woman—neither of the "painted doll" type that enlisted men reviled, nor the shallow and vain sort that Charles King often lampooned in his popular novels of the frontier army. Ellen was well read and strove to obtain the best possible education for her children. She enrolled John and David in a private boarding school in Connecticut in 1875, even though it meant a six-year separation from them. Nellie attended secondary school at Ellicott City, Maryland, under the tutelage of Sarah Randolph, one of the foremost educators of her day, then went on to college at Radcliffe. Son Nicholas enrolled at Harvard in 1894.

David Harmony Biddle would make his father proud, first by volunteering for military service during the Philippine Insurrection, and then by accepting a regular commission as a first lieutenant in the 6th U.S. Cavalry in 1901. But it was Nellie whose life bore the fullest testimony to her mother's good parenting. After graduating from Radcliffe, she married Louis Evan Shipman, a young writer from Brooklyn. In the summer of 1893 the couple moved to Cornish, New Hampshire, a part of the literary and artistic set that founded the "Cornish Colony." With the money her husband made from a story, *The Curious Courtship of Kate Pins*, they bought an old brick tavern house in nearby Plainfield Village. Louis went on to become a popular playwright, and his works appeared regularly on Broadway between 1901 and 1922.

Ellen McGowan Biddle Shipman enjoyed the Cornish Art Colony immensely, so much so that she staked a permanent claim to a Cornish address, writing on the reverse of one of her calling cards, "geographically in Plainfield, socially in Cornish." It was at the Cornish Colony, while dabbling in gardening, that Ellen displayed a talent for landscape architecture. With the encouragement of noted architect Charles Platt, in 1914 she accepted a job in Grosse Pointe, Michigan, to redo a garden that Platt had originally designed. Her work was a rousing success. Over the next thirty-three years she would design some 650 gardens from coast to coast, rising to the top of a then male-dominated profession and becoming recognized as the foremost American woman landscape architect of the twentieth century.

Reminiscences of a Soldier's Wife has much to recommend it. Ellen McGowan Biddle wrote in a clear, pleasant, and conversational style perfectly suited to the subject matter. Despite a self-confessed tendency toward hero worship, Ellen offers good glimpses into the characters of generals William T. Sherman and August V. Kautz, as well as many of the lower-ranking officers with whom her husband served. A detailed and faithful picture of domestic life at frontier army posts also emerges from the work. Where Ellen faltered was in her sense of time. When writing of major events, both public and personal, she is vague on precise dates and at times neglects to give even approximate ones. I will try to rectify this shortcoming with the following chronological summary of the Biddle's lives from 1866–1907, the period described in *Reminiscences of a Soldier's Wife*.

In August 1866, nineteen-year-old Ellen McGowan Biddle left New York with her two infant sons to join her husband at Macon, Georgia, the headquarters of the newly consti-tuted 24th U.S. Infantry. Captain Biddle had been ordered to Macon six months earlier. From Macon, Biddle was transferred to Natchez, and then to Jackson, Mississippi.

In April 1869, the 24th and 29th Infantry regiments were consolidated into the 11th Infantry. Biddle and his new regiment were assigned to Reconstruction duty at Bren-ham, Texas. Unable to tolerate life there, ("I had a horror of Texas and was not very well"), Ellen returned to her parents' home after three or four months. Captain Biddle joined her on an extended leave of absence in the autumn of 1869, in time for the birth of their daughter, Nellie.

Biddle's leave expired at the end of December 1870, and he departed to join his new regiment, the 1st U.S. Cavalry, at Benicia Barracks, California. Ellen remained with her parents "some months, growing stronger every day and bet-ter fitted for the frontier life that was before [me]." Her hus-band, meanwhile, was transferred to Camp Halleck, Nevada, and in mid-1871 she joined him there. Late the following year she miscarried and fell seriously ill. When she had recovered enough to travel, Captain Biddle took her to the Presidio of San Francisco to convalesce.

In January 1873, James left Ellen to join his regiment in action against the Modoc Indians in the Lava Beds of northern California. Their nine-year-old son David accompanied him. While on campaign Biddle received a promotion to major of the 6th U.S. Cavalry. The 6th was stationed elsewhere, but Brig. Gen. Edward R. S. Canby, the department commander, prevailed upon Major Biddle to remain in the Lava Beds as a member of his staff. Biddle and his young son saw the Modoc campaign through to its end in June 1873.

At the request of the commander of the Department of the Missouri, Brig. Gen. John Pope, Major Biddle took charge of Fort Lyon, a comparatively large post that was garrisoned with four companies of infantry and two troops of the 6th Cavalry.

In August 1874, Biddle and his troops departed Fort Lyon for extended duty under Col. Nelson A. Miles in the Red River War. After a few months alone with the children at Fort Lyon, Ellen took them east to her parents' home. Major Biddle applied for leave in December 1874. Although he had been on continuous duty for four years, the request was denied. Instead, Biddle was assigned command of a cantonment on the Sweetwater River in the Indian Territory.

At the conclusion of the Red River War in June 1875, Biddle was granted four months' leave. He had been separated from his family for sixteen months. Recalled Ellen, "It was a great joy to his old father, who had not long to live, to see him again, and we made plans for a pleasant summer." Major Biddle had been home only a few weeks when, on July 9, 1875, orders came for him to report to his regiment in Arizona. Ellen elected to stay behind and put her two boys in school.

Ellen set out for Arizona in January 1876 with Nellie. As her husband was on campaign against hostile Apaches,

Ellen passed the winter in San Francisco. James came for them in March, and after a miserable journey they reached Fort Whipple, the department headquarters, in April. There Biddle was detailed to staff duty as inspector general of the Department of Arizona. In December 1880, he returned to a line command, at Fort Grant in southern Arizona. Four years later, Ellen left Fort Grant for Philadelphia, to see her sons John and David for the first time in six years. She took a summer cottage at Virginia Springs for her health in July 1885. A month later, her daughter Alice died of a sudden illness. Ellen passed the fall and winter of 1885 in Elizabeth, New Jersey with her sister and her brother-in-law, Commodore Harmony, then on duty at the Navy Department.

In 1886, Major Biddle was ordered east and took up quarters with his family at Fort Myers, Virginia. He had not seen his eldest sons in nine years. The following year Biddle received an assignment to the War Department and, on October 19, 1887, a promotion to the lieutenant colonelcy of the 5th U.S. Cavalry. Biddle joined the regiment in Colorado in April 1890. Ellen went to the mountains of West Virginia for her health, and they remained apart for three years. The "outdoor life in that healthful region, superintending work of building our home, completely restored my health," said Ellen, and in the spring of 1894 she joined her husband at Fort Robinson, Nebraska. Biddle had been promoted to the colonelcy of the 9th U.S. Cavalry on July 1, 1891. Ellen was delighted with Fort Robinson; not only was it a large garrison, but the couple also had indoor plumbing for the first time in their long years of frontier duty.

Colonel Biddle was retired for age on December 11, 1896. Their departure from Fort Robinson and the 9th

Cavalry Buffalo Soldiers, said Ellen, was one of the saddest of her life. The couple settled at Berkeley Springs, West Virginia, and in 1904, Biddle had the satisfaction of being advanced to brigadier general on the retired list.

General Biddle died on June 9, 1910, three years after Ellen's *Reminiscences of a Soldier's Wife* was published. He was buried in Section 3 of Arlington National Cemetery. Ellen followed him in death twelve years later. She lies in an adjacent plot at Arlington.

Ellen forever remained proud of her husband, the army, and the small part she played in making frontier duty tolerable for James Biddle and the men of his commands. "I am but a woman," she wrote plaintively, "but I have helped bear the burden and heat of the day."

To those wishing to read other books by women who went west with the army after the Civil War, I suggest the titles listed below. For each, I have given both the original publication data and that of the most recent reprint.

Boyd, Mrs. Orasmus B. (Frances Anne). *Cavalry Life in Tent and Field* (New York: J. Selwin Tate and Sons, 1894; reprint, Lincoln: University of Nebraska Press, 1982).

Carrington, Frances C. *My Army Life and the Fort Phil Kearney Massacre* (Philadelphia: J. B. Lippincott Company, 1910, reprint, Boulder, Co.: Pruett Publishing Company, 1993).

Carrington, Margaret I. *Ab-Sa-Ra-Ka, Home of the Crows* (Philadelphia: J. B. Lippincott and Company, 1868; reprint, Lincoln: University of Nebraska Press, 1983).

Fougera, Katherine A. *With Custer's Cavalry: From the Memoirs of the Late Katherine Gibson* (Caldwell, Idaho: The

Caxton Printers, 1940; reprint, Lincoln: University of
Nebraska Press, 1986).

Roe, Frances M. *Army Letters from an Officer's Wife, 1871-
1888* (New York: Appleton, 1909; reprint, Lincoln:
University of Nebraska Press, 1981).

Summerhayes, Martha. *Vanished Arizona: Recollections of the
Army Life of a New England Woman* (Philadelphia: J. B.
Lippincott, 1908; reprint, Alexandria, Va.: Time-Life
Books, 1981).

Ellen McGowan Biddle's *Reminiscences of a Soldier's Wife*
is alone among these outstanding memoirs of frontier army
wives in having not been reprinted until now. First editions
are scarce and expensive, generally bringing between $150
and $200 in good condition. The appearance of *Reminis-
cences of a Soldier's Wife* as a part of Stackpole's Frontier Clas-
sics series makes this charming and important title again
available to a wide audience.

PREFACE

Sitting on a rose-covered porch, with the odour of jessamine, heliotrope and magnolia all about me, my thoughts went back to the delightful days of my life spent in Mississippi; the inspiration came upon me to write the reminiscences of my army life beginning in that beloved State.

E. McG. B.

Santa Barbara, California.

List of Illustrations

" Never set sail to fear :
  Come into port grandly
Or sail the seas with God."

Reminiscences of
a Soldier's Wife

CHAPTER I.

On a bright Autumn day not many years after the
close of the great Civil War, I started with my two
sons on the steamer "Flambeau," commanded by
Captain Alfred Everson, from New York to Savannah, to join my husband, Captain James Biddle,
U.S.A., who was then stationed at Macon, Georgia.
The sea was as smooth as glass; great flocks of sociable
gulls, each with a drop of water always on his bill,
swarmed around to catch what might be thrown from
the boat, and I and the little ones,—one fourteen
months old, and the other barely two months—having
been put under the captain's special care by my
father and brother-in-law, Captain Harmony, who
were both sailors and knew the good sea qualities,
also the good war record, of the captain, found the

voyage delightful. Jack, the elder, ran about the ship taking care of himself, much to the amusement of the passengers, while Dave was such a splendid specimen of health and good humor he knew not what it was to be cross, so we were not avoided by our fellow-travellers, but on the contrary we received the greatest courtesy and kindness.

On arriving at Savannah the children and I were dressed ready to go ashore, and went on deck to see the captain bring the good ship into port. The dock was crowded with men and women who had come to meet their friends; I glanced over the crowd and soon saw my husband was not one of them. I was very young and inexperienced and suddenly felt myself growing ill; I knew no more, for I had fainted, falling on the deck of the steamer. An English gentleman passenger, a stranger, kindly picked me up and carried me to the captain's room, tenderly laid me on a couch, and then summoned the ship's surgeon. I was speedily brought to my senses and to the realisation that I was alone in a strange city with two infants, and a nurse scarcely older than myself. As soon as the captain got his ship made fast and had a moment he came to me. His great big sailor heart soon showed out, and he began to make plans for me. He telegraphed to Macon and soon arrangements were made for our journey, for

12

I insisted upon going that evening. My husband had been detained at the last moment, being a member of a court-martial. He had telegraphed an officer stationed in Savannah asking him to meet me and make arrangements to send us to Macon; but either the ship got in earlier than was expected, or the officer forgot us. I like to give him the benefit of the doubt.

After an early dinner on the "Flambeau" (for the captain would not let us go to the hotel), he took me for a drive, to see the city with its lovely gardens, Pulaski Park of historic memory, and the beautiful old cemetery, Buena Vista. The city was regularly laid out with broad streets, and there were innumerable small parks, one at almost every corner; it was a lovely drive, and the captain's kind thoughtfulness in trying to make me forget my trouble made such an impression upon me that I have never forgotten the day. He passed into the unknown many years ago. *"Requiescat in pace."*

About sundown we started for Macon, travelling at night as the day trains were very slow, stopping at almost every hamlet; the cars were small and old, the road-bed very poor, and there were no sleeping-cars. As the night time came on it grew very cold and damp; in fact I have never suffered more with cold than I did on that journey, and greatly feared

13

my children would be made ill. However, as I said before, they were perfectly healthful and stood the night better than I did, for I had taken my warm wraps to cover them, and being far from strong and my anxiety great lest something serious had happened to prevent the Colonel from meeting me, passed a sleepless night. In the morning we were met at the station by my husband (who was always called "Colonel" from having held that rank during the war, and hereafter I shall call him by that title). He had never seen his second son, and I was very proud to show him the fine boy.

Six months previous, when the Colonel had been ordered to Macon, it was thought best for me and my young child "Jack" not to go south for the summer; besides, I was scarcely well enough at that time to take a long fatiguing journey, but now we had safely arrived, and all of our troubles were forgotten. We went to the hotel to rest a few days while the Colonel put a few last finishing touches to the little cabin that was to be our home. The garrison, where many of the officers and their families lived, was three miles from the city; it was very small, and there were no quarters for another family, so the Colonel had secured a small cabin (that had been used as negro quarters before the war) which was near the garrison. After it had been thoroughly

14

cleaned with several coats of good sweet whitewash, it was made habitable, and when we got the little furniture we owned into it (for the Government allowed an officer but a few hundred pounds of freight), a few household gods that I always had about me, and a great big fire on the hearth, we had our first Army Home.

I soon got an old black Mammy for cook and she took care of "all youse chillins," as she called me and the babies, and with the white nurse, Sally, that I had taken from home, we got along fairly well. The life was entirely new to me, but I soon discovered that I had adaptability, which made things easier. I was entirely without luxuries and comforts, and had many privations, but all of the army ladies had the same discomforts, though there were few complaints, and never by a thoroughbred. The war had desolated the whole surrounding country.

Our little cabin of four rooms stood alone in a large field about one hundred feet from a high embankment along which a railway ran. I was alone with my children most of the day except when the ladies and the officers of the garrison came in to see me. They were very kind (as I afterward learned most army women are), telling me what to do and how to do it, for I had much to learn; the officers came often to luncheon or dinner. Sometimes we would go in the kitchen and cook all kinds of things from receipt-books, as our amusements were few and the good things to eat fewer; there were not many first-class cooks to be found there. The first of my chafing-dish cooking that was years later so popular on the frontier, I learned at Macon. Often two or three of the young lieutenants and myself would get up a nice little supper and invite the older officers and their wives, and they generally pronounced them very good.

I well remember the first Christmas in the garrison. We invited all the officers and their families who lived at the hotel, as well as the young bachelor officers who were in the garrison, to dine with us. The carpenter made us a long table of boards nailed to wooden horses. We all sat on benches, except the Colonel and General Ruger, who commanded the district. The room was hung with evergreen and holly, which grows in great profusion in that climate. Old Mammy cooked us a delicious dinner under my directions, for my dear mother had insisted upon my learning to cook when I had decided to marry a soldier; for she realized the privations I would have to undergo much better than I did, as up to that time I had hardly had a serious thought. Our dinner was fine. We had two roasted turkeys and a fine tender goose, a champagned ham, lettuce salad, and an Old

16

English plum-pudding, which my mother had sent
from home. All of the dinner was put upon the table.
The young officers—God bless them, many now lying
in honored graves—served us when we could not help
ourselves. Colonel Wykoff, who was killed long after
at San Juan Hill, was one of those dear fellows. It
was a very happy day, and I love to look back and
recall those first days of my garrison experience.
There were no conventionalities; life was very simple
and the young officer looked up to his superiors
with respect and admiration, trying to emulate
them; for all of the older ones had distinguished
themselves on the field of battle.

I also recall the first time I went to church in
Macon, about three miles distant. I went alone, in
the old Government ambulance, drawn by two mules.
When I reached the church door there were many
people standing about, especially men and young boys,
and I felt myself "the observed of all observers." I
approached the church door with a beating heart, for
I had heard of many acts of discourtesy being shown
to Union people; but I went in and found a seat for
myself, and enjoyed the beautiful service, forgetting
for the time that I was not in my old "Saint John's,"
of Revolutionary date, in Elizabeth, New Jersey. The
next Sunday, when I again went in the same old
ambulance, I was politely met at the church door and

given a seat in the front of the church. I afterward became acquainted with the rector and his charming wife, and made many friends in that delightful town of cultivated people, and although I lived there but four months we came to know and to understand the people well and I was sorry when the order came for us to go to Natchez, Mississippi.

After the receipt of the order for the change of station, we were very busy breaking up the little home. The cabin was soon dismantled, and soldiers packed the furniture, mattresses going into a long box that had served for a divan, and other things going into boxes that had been used as dressing-tables, washstands, tables, etc., etc. We were allowed but fourteen hundred pounds of freight, and we learned to utilize everything. The packing was soon done and good-byes said to all of our friends, including the dear old black Mammy, with genuine regret. It seemed very sad to me to leave the regiment, every one of whom had been so kind to me; and one of them, Mrs. John Wilkins, seeing the tears in my eyes, said: "Oh, you must be a better soldier; it is only an *au revoir;* we will soon meet again," yet it was many years before we saw each other and then in Arizona, where she was ever most kind to me and to my little ones born there, taking the place of my mother. She, too, has passed beyond.

18

We left Macon (on the same little old cars that had taken us there) for Mobile, Alabama. The journey during the day was uneventful; the whole country was in a terrible condition from the armies passing and repassing over it for several years, and it would have been hard then to believe that it ever could be as flourishing as it is now. On reaching Dalonaga, Georgia, we found the trains went no further; and as the roads and country generally were in such bad condition it was considered unsafe to travel at night, so we were obliged to go to the primitive little hotel to remain until morning. The house was about three hundred yards from the station. We had to pass up through an avenue of trees. The Colonel took Jack, who was now a fine, sturdy little lad, wearing a blue pilot-cloth overcoat with pockets in it (much to his delight), which the sailors on board of the receiving-ship "Vermont" had made him during our visit to Lieutenant and Mrs. Harmony at the New York Navy-yard. While there we had the great pleasure of meeting Admiral Farragut, who seemed very fond of my children and often took Jack by the hand for a walk around the navy-yard. He was also greatly interested in the christening of my little son David, and gave me some water brought from the river Jordan for the purpose, also a bottle of fine old Madeira which he had brought

19

from the island years before when a midship-
man. I love to think that my sons have felt the
kindly touch of this great man's hand. The Admiral
dearly loved children, and I have observed since then
that all great men have simple natures and a strong
love for the little ones in their hearts.

But to return to Dalonaga, where the Colonel
had Jack by the hand, the nurse carrying Dave, and
I bringing up the rear with the carriage-blanket. It
was quite dark when we arrived at the station, and,
as I have said, the avenue was lined with trees, so
that it was now perfectly dark; a man went ahead
carrying a lantern, while we all followed after. Soon
after we started I surprised myself by walking into
a hole that had been dug for a gate-post, which
must have been five feet deep, and notwithstanding
I called several times I could not be heard and the
party went on without me. When the travellers
arrived at the house and the Colonel was counting
his little flock, he found, to his great consternation,
one missing; so the old man with the lantern and he
started out for a hunt. I was soon located at the
bottom of the hole, and with the help of both was
drawn up to *terra firma*. Our troubles did not end
here. We were told our train was due at seven A.M.
but about four o'clock we were awakened by loud
knocking at our door, and a man saying that our train

20

was due in thirty minutes. Such a time as we had getting ourselves and the children dressed, and with a nurse, too, who had not under difficulties, developed adaptability. On going down stairs ready to start we were coolly informed that "the man had made a mistake; thought we were going on the north-bound." I have always been thankful that there was no murder committed that morning.

We reached Mobile safely, notwithstanding the dirty old cars and bad road-bed. We went to the hotel to remain a day or two, where we found our old friend Colonel Ned Hudson, one of the handsomest men in the army, was in command of the garrison. He was very glad to see us, insisted upon our going to his house, and could not have been kinder, and we soon found all the Southern people in his department were devoted to him. He was a most courtly, elegant gentleman, as well as a fine soldier. It has been told of his brother and himself, that when they were travelling in Germany they went to see the maneuvers of the army. Emperor William I, seeing these wonderfully handsome men, both about six feet three inches tall, and with splendid physique, sent one of his aides-de-camp to inquire who they were; on hearing that one was an American army officer, he sent for them and showed them every attention during their stay.

Well, I greatly enjoyed the visit to Mobile. The ground on which the city is built gradually rises as it goes back from the river, and there are high hills back of the city where many of the residents go for the summer. The streets were beautifully shaded, and all had gardens. Among other pleasures was a delightful horseback ride with several officers out on the shell road, where we stopped and had a cup of tea and other little dainties. We also went out to the entrance of the bay. I was most anxious to see where Farragut ran past Forts Morgan and Gaines, and destroyed the Confederate fleet, one member of my family having been with the Union fleet. The few days were filled with delightful excitement and of course I was sorry to leave, but go we must, and we left for New Orleans.

Nothing of interest occurred, the country being as desolated as in Georgia, and I was glad when we reached the city, where we spent two or three days waiting for the boat. Here we met some old friends, dined with the dear Marstons, and met Mrs. Shaw, Mrs. Marston's charming mother, who belonged to one of the old Creole families. We also drove out to Jackson Barracks, on the Mississippi River. It was a beautiful place, with wonderful old oak trees covered with hanging moss; the officers' quarters were excellent (compared to the cabin we had lived in).

22

We had tea with Captain and Mrs. Graham, and most delicious strawberries; I had not seen Mrs. Graham since she was a child in Elizabeth, New Jersey, where her father, General Ricketts, a most distinguished officer of our army, lived. Mrs. Graham married when very young, scarcely sixteen years old. It was a great pleasure to meet her again, also her husband, now General William M. Graham. Every one there seemed glad to see us. There were many old friends of the Colonel and they begged us to stay a few days—dear, warm-hearted army people! We could not accept their hospitality, the Colonel being under orders, and I could not think of visiting with two babies. While in New Orleans we went to see Port Hudson; saw the fortifications where the gallant Farragut had a fight in which the frigate "Mississippi" was burned, of which the present Admiral Dewey was executive officer. These naval battles were always most interesting to me. I had heard the officers talk them over with my father at home, and my brother-in-law, Lieutenant Harmony, was on the "Iroquois."

We also went to see the French Market, another interesting sight. There were several buildings of unusual architecture, and one would think from the number of languages heard spoken that people from all over the world had brought their wares for sale.

23

The display of flowers was most beautiful. I have never since seen it equalled. The day we left we went to Lake Pontchartrain and had luncheon with some friends, so I was well tired out when we took the "General Quitman," one of the magnificent boats that ran on the river at that time, for Natchez, about two hundred and eighty miles up the river. The boat was commanded by a famous man, Captain Leathers, who was killed after an eventful life, many years after we had left that part of the country.

After being on board a short time we found we were not *persona grata;* the Colonel, being in uniform, had many black looks, and the people generally on the boat stood aloof from the Yankees, but there was much to be seen that was new to me—the beautiful plantations that lined both sides of the river, the numerous boats passing of every description, the landing of our own boat at the plantations, and the singing of the negroes as they discharged and took on cargo. So the day soon passed, and when the night time came we had forgotten we had been ostracised. During the night I was awakened by the stewardess, who apologised for calling me; she said a lady on the boat who had a young babe had been taken desperately ill the afternoon before; her babe, whom she nursed, would not take the bottle and was crying with hunger. The stewardess had seen me

24

nurse my fine boy and wondered if I would be willing
to nurse the poor little infant. It was not long before
the dear little babe had satisfied the pangs of hunger
and was sweetly sleeping in my arms; it slept the
night through; and by arranging matters I had the
pleasure of nursing both the little ones for about
twelve hours.

The second day we were on the boat I was greatly
surprised when two of the ladies, who had seemed to
be afraid of my coming too close to them, came to
me and regretted they had not met me the day before.
Of course, I was amused, but received them kindly, as
the victor can always receive the vanquished; never-
theless I wondered why I was received to-day when I
was disdained yesterday, but soon learned that the
stewardess of the boat had told some ladies that I
had nursed the child, and the mother instinct was
too strong in them; they felt that I was as human as
they, though I had come from the North. Our passage
after that was delightful, showing how ready these
distressed people were to yield to kindness.

Every night there was music and dancing aboard
until midnight. Each boat always carried a fine
band, which also played at luncheon and dinner.
There were games and charades, the latter being much
in vogue at that time; while below, many of the men
passengers played cards, and I was told that thou-

sands of dollars often exchanged hands. It was altogether a new experience for me, and like the Lotus Eaters, I sailed along forgetful of the morrow; enjoying each day as it came, bringing new scenes into my life, as well as new thoughts into my mind. The awakening was when we reached Natchez, and I began to realise that life was real.

An amusing incident had occurred before we left the boat. Several rough men on the lower deck talked in a loud voice about "the war and the South being overpowered, but not conquered, and if she had the chance she would do it again." The Colonel paid no attention whatever to them, but was amused, for he well knew that the fighters on both sides were glad to lay down their arms. At one place on the river some cattle had to be landed. They all went off quietly except one steer, who positively refused to leave the boat; finally the poor thing was thrown down and bound with ropes, and after much pulling and hauling the steer was landed; when, to the surprise of everyone, a man, leaning over the rail, who had had a good many drinks, called out when he saw the steer reach the ground: "Overpowered, but not conquered. She'll do it again if you give her a chance." It is almost useless to say we heard nothing further about the South from the roughs.

CHAPTER II.

WE reached Natchez, under the hill, on a bright
Sunday morning. The city was built on a high bluff,
nearly two hundred feet above the river. We had
to drive up a winding road from the boat. The streets
were beautifully shaded, like all the Southern cities
we had passed through, and the lovely china-trees
were in full bloom, and the odour of the blossom was
delicious. We went to the little hotel until the
Colonel could go to the fort and see if there were any
accommodations for us to live there. While he was
gone an officer, Lieutenant Gray, called on me. He
said he was glad the Colonel had arrived, and
although the houses at the fort were hardly habitable,
he hoped they could be put in order, so that we might
live there, etc., etc. All the time he talked I saw he
was watching me and that something was on his mind.

The old fort at Natchez was above the city on the
outskirts. It had been the beautiful home of the
Surzet family. The "residence" (as fine houses are
always called in the South) had been pulled down
during the war and a large earthwork enclosing about
ten acres of ground was thrown up. The entrance

was over a causeway through a gate, where a sentinel always walked; the guard-house was just inside the gate. The house we occupied was a cabin, formerly used by the negroes of the Surzet family, and was about sixty yards from the guard-house. There were no large guns, all having been removed; but the magazines were intact—large rooms covered with earth. The soldiers' quarters were long two-story buildings, near the bluff on the river; there was also a little old cabin on the bluff, where I used to sit and watch the boats. I soon learned their different lights and whistles and could tell at night what boat was passing. We soon got the little cabins in order. We had two under one roof, each with two rooms; on one side was the living-room and dining-room, and on the other side two bedrooms. The kitchen was detached from the house.

When the Colonel first joined the Eleventh Infantry, then stationed at Natchez, to which he had been transferred in the consolidation of regiments after the war, there was a very disorderly, rough set of men in the army and there was constant fighting and trouble in the two companies now under the Colonel's command. He told the first sergeant the next fight that occurred to call him immediately; there were two or three "bullies" who were the ringleaders and caused all the trouble. One evening the sergeant came hastily and reported a fight in the quarters. Colonel buckled on his sword and was off in a moment. He found two of these bullies had knocked down and hurt a couple of peaceful men and a general fight had ensued. The Colonel was a man weighing two hundred pounds, was an athlete and tremendously strong; he greatly surprised them when he picked up one of the big fellows and threw him out of the quarters and the other followed in a second after. The sergeant was on hand at the door with some men, and the two ringleaders were put in the guard-house. The next morning the Colonel made them walk the earthworks in a barrel with the head and bottom knocked out and a heavy log of wood across their shoulders. When they found they had a master they gave up, and the Colonel had no more trouble in the command. Drastic measures had to be used in those days. The men, both foreign and domestic, were a hard set; not at all the class of men we now have in the army.

The town was very orderly, and in every way things went smoothly, and after the military duties of the morning were over we rode horseback. The country was beautiful, and the gates of the numerous plantations were left open and we could ride through them from one to the other. The Colonel also had charge of the Freedman's Bureau, which had been established March 3, 1865, by Congress passing an act organizing in the War Department the bureau of refugees, freedmen and abandoned lands. It was known as the Freedman's Bureau, and remained in operation until January 1, 1869. The number of rations issued to the colored people during that time was over fifteen million and it cost the Government $14,996,480. All this work was under the supervision of army officers, in addition to their other duties, the Colonel having six counties under his command. Often on our rides he combined duty with pleasure in going over his department.

We had been at Natchez but a few months when a petition was sent from some men, ("carpet-baggers" who had gone from the North to try and secure political places,) to General Gillem, commanding the district, asking for a reversal of one of Judge Shields' decisions. The case was referred to the Colonel for an opinion and report. He carefully examined the same and sent his report to the General, sustaining the Judge. When the papers were returned the Colonel went to the court-room and handed the decision of General Gillem to the Judges, who complimented Colonel Biddle on the clear and impressive endorsement that had evidently caused the decision of the General commanding. After this the people could not do enough for us. They found the Colonel just and were willing to abide by his decisions, and all that section of the country, in the Freedman's Bureau, reconstruction and in all other respects, was soon settled, and the people were beginning to forget there had been such a bitter war.

One day later a carriage drove up to our cabin. Colonel and I were sitting out-of-doors on the porch, —though there was no roof to it and the few narrow boards lay flat on the ground.

An elderly gentleman and lady alighted and came towards us; the Colonel rose to receive them; they introduced themselves and paid us a delightful visit. A few days after the gentleman (Judge Shields) called again and begged us to live in one of his "residences," on a plantation about a mile from the town, which was vacant. He was so gentlemanly and put the matter in such a way that it made him the indebted one to us, instead of our being indebted to him for a comfortable home. He said he and his wife had been very unhappy since their call, seeing me and my children living in the negro quarters belonging to one of their relations. We accepted their hospitality and in a few days I moved out with the nurses, the children, the cook, the coachman, horses, dogs, and of course the Colonel's fighting cocks, for they had to have the best of everything!

The place was beautiful. I had never seen a

31

finer house or garden, and was delighted. The nurse
helped me to unpack and put the clothes in the
bureau-drawers and closets. The Colonel came home
after retreat and left early in the morning. I stayed
there just two days. The stillness and lonesomeness
nearly killed me. The little ones were out all day,
except when sleeping, and I could not stand the
silence. I had been one of a large family and accustomed to a large house; though not so elegant, it was
filled with gay laughter and joyful sounds. I became
so homesick that I moved back to the little cabin.

Shortly after this a fire occurred in the fort, and
it was with great difficulty kept from reaching the
magazines. The Colonel decided he would move us
to a furnished house in town near, and where he could
be with us oftener and his mind relieved, having us
away from the dangers and unpleasantnesses of the
fort. During the time I lived there and all the while
we were stationed at Natchez I was the only lady
belonging to the garrison, and many days when the
Colonel had to be away life seemed very quiet after
the gay household of girls I have spoken of.

The officers belonging to my husband's company
were Lieutenants John L. Churchill and Max Wesendorf. The former was most delightful, a graduate
of Columbia College; he came into the army at the
close of the war. He was clever, well-read, quick at

repartee, and altogether a delightful companion, as well as being greatly interested in his duties and anxious to be a good soldier. He is dead; and although he did not die on the field of battle, he gave his life to his country, for he died from the effects of climate while stationed in the South, which was most unhealthful at that period. I often think how greatly he brightened the days spent in that forlorn little cabin. Often the Colonel had to be gone several hours attending to business of the Freedman's Bureau. Lieutenant Churchill would always look after us and have some pleasant diversion to pass the time.

Lieutenant Wesendorf was a German, as his name indicates, his father being a General in the Prussian army. At the outbreak of the Civil War Mr. Wesendorf joined our army, as many foreigners did, and, distinguishing himself, was given a commission. He was a good officer as well as a good soldier, which is not always the case.

These gentlemen took their meals with us, as there was no place for them to go and no place that could be used as a kitchen in their quarters. They both lived in one little cabin, an iron bedstead, table, washstand and a couple of chairs constituting the furniture of their rooms. Mr. Wesendorf was devotedly fond of my son David; and on one occasion, when I was going away for a few days, he asked: "If you should not return, will you give me Dave?" which was cheerful, as I was not very strong at the time. Dave was now about eight months old and had an old black Mammy for a nurse. One day, when I was not well, the Colonel went out to the kitchen to see the child. It was the servants' dinner hour. He found Dave sucking a great piece of 'possum, the grease fairly running off his elbows. He exclaimed: "Lucy, what do you mean by giving the child that meat?" Lucy said: "Why, Lord bless your soul, Massa Colonel, he's bin eatin' 'possum for months; it don't hurt him, it makes him grow." Certainly Dave was the picture of health, and the biggest child of his age I ever saw; so perhaps the 'possum did not hurt him; but I should hardly prescribe it as a baby's diet.

As I have said, we soon moved to town and had a nice little house and garden. The Colonel had become a great favorite in the town with the men, and the women were coming to see me. We were invited to luncheons, dinners, and receptions, all of which pleased me very much; for I had not gone into society before my marriage (being considered too young) and I thought it delightful. I had good servants; Becky, the cook, also did the marketing. Caroline, a light mulatto, was the head nurse, and a more faithful creature never lived; she was a most

34

accomplished maid, very responsible and reliable in
every way. She lived with me a number of years
and then had to return to the South (on a small pension), on account of her health. It was a great grief
to me and the boys when we had to give her up.
Thornton, our coachman, was also a good reliable man.
They were all negroes and had been slaves, raised in
the families in and about Natchez. We got them all
when we moved to the town; they were recommended
by our friends, who had been on the lookout for
them for us. Owing to them, my household cares
were few; a visit to the kitchen and old Becky in the
morning with the *menu* for twenty-four hours was
all I had to do in that department, and Caroline
looked after the rest of the house; so I was able to
be out-of-doors most of the day, generally riding
horseback in the morning, and driving in the afternoon with the children and nurses or making calls.

The life was delightful, and some of the warmest
and dearest friends of my life were then made. We
often went fox hunting, getting up early in the morning to be off before day. We would hear the horn
singing, ''A southerly wind and clouded sky proclaim
it a hunting morning.'' No gate or bars stopped me
in those days. Often the Colonel was scared seeing
me take them, but I never had an accident. Many
years later I came near having one, having mounted a

bucking horse, but with assistance got off without accident. Cock-fighting was a favorite pastime of the gentlemen of Natchez and the South, and my husband, being somewhat of a sporting man, always had fine birds and was ready to join them. I well remember one day when Mr. Minor was to have a main. The gentlemen from town had taken their birds out in their carriages to his plantation, when it began to rain; so they all adjourned to his *wife's parlour,* she being in New Orleans at the time. I often wondered what was the final result of that main.

I must not forget to say that the Colonel was able to get money from the Government for the rent of the ground where the fort stood from the time the war ceased. Mrs. Surzet, from being very wealthy, had become poor. She had lost her slaves; her house and property had been taken for a fort, and the house was demolished. It seemed only just that she should have rent for the ground after the war ceased.

Although I was born south of Mason and Dixon's line, I was not old enough when my parents moved North to remember anything about it; but the outdoor life, the grand old oaks with the hanging moss, the wonderful bloom of the flowers, particularly the camellias and japonicas, which I had never before seen, appealed to me greatly. Often flat baskets filled with these exquisite flowers were sent me, their deli-

"MONMOUTH," NATCHEZ, MISSISSIPPI, THE HOME OF GENERAL QUITMAN

cate stems being stuck in wet sand, and somehow they always reminded me of beautiful white doves.

There is but one unpleasant memory connected with my life in this dear city, and that is, I had the yellow fever. I had not the least fear of the disease, though the Colonel was fearful for us and had taken a house in the country. We were just about to move, when I came in from a drive with a headache, and, though it was unusual, the thought of the fever did not occur to me and I continued our preparations to move; until I felt so badly that I thought I would go into the parlour, where it was cool and quiet, and lie down on the big old-fashioned sofa. How long I was there I never knew. Lieutenant Wesendorf came in to dinner about two o'clock and found me lying there unconscious, picked me up and carried me into the Colonel's room on the other side of the hall, where he was in bed with the dengue or break-bone fever. In an instant he was out of bed, and Wesendorf went on his horse as fast as possible for the post surgeon, Dr. Gillet. It was soon discovered that I had the fever. The children and nurses were sent away. A fire was made on my hearth and the windows in both rooms were opened and kept open, having a current of air with the bedstead entirely out of the draught. The doctor never left the house until I was convalescent. He and my husband took turns in getting a little sleep. It took me a long while to recover from the effects of that dreaded and dreadful disease, and I always thought I never looked quite the same after it. The freshness of youth was gone, but my life was saved, and neither of my children or my faithful servants took the disease and I was thankful.

I must not forget to say that the yellow fever was brought into Natchez by a peddler. The Colonel had quarantined Natchez against all boats coming from New Orleans and the South. This peddler got off the boat some miles below and walked to the city, where he fell in the street and died, and it was found he had died of the fever. Hundreds of cases and many deaths was the result.

I remember one day passing a shop, kept by Mr. Carradine, and seeing a beautiful blue-and-white French organdie muslin, which I greatly admired. My husband asked: "Don't you want it?" but I had just received a box of gowns from Sophie in New Orleans and felt I did not need it. Still he tempted me, saying: "If you will make it yourself, I will not only buy the material, but you can buy any Valenciennes lace you may want to trim it with." He well knew my weakness; there was nothing I loved so much as a bit of lace—real filmy, beautiful old lace. I hesitated, however, remembering so well the time when first married he gave me a twenty-dollar gold piece (when gold was scarce) if I would make a plain calico dress for myself. Unfortunately, I took the pay in advance. Many times I threw the thing down, declaring I would try no more to finish it; when the Colonel would quietly say: "But you have spent the twenty dollars;" and I would go to work again. He was anxious for me to learn to sew, knowing I might have it to do sometime when away from civilisation, as we were apt to be. The lace tempted me and the materials were bought. (The lace I have to this day.) Fortunately for me, just at this time the beautiful Mrs. Marston came to visit us (with her dear little Clarisse), and under her directions the gown was built and was a thing of beauty for many years, and greatly admired. The making of it developed a latent talent, for afterward, when we lived on the frontier and I could not have sewing of any kind done, with the help of the nurse I made everything that my children and I wore. So the Colonel did not lose greatly in the end, and I was benefited.

We had been at Natchez nearly two years when one day the Colonel came in hastily and said: "Orders have come for the command to go to Jackson, Mississippi. Can you be ready in twenty-four hours to move?" Of course, I could, and was. Some men from the company came and packed the little furniture we had.

We were living in a furnished house, and it did not take long to pack silver, glass, china, books, and our clothes. When it became known that we were to leave, there was universal regret, every one thinking the carpet-baggers had succeeded in having the Colonel removed as they had never ceased trying, and reported to Washington that the Colonel was too intimate and too lenient to the Southern people, completely forgetting that the war was over; but the Colonel was being ordered to a more important command. Everything was peaceful here, and the troops had to go where they were needed. Among the notes received,—of condolence, I was about to say,—one came from Mrs. Henry, a most charming woman, who had a young girls' school. She wrote: "It is said that when stout old Martin Luther was irritable or tempted to be cast down by the successful machinations of enemies, or anything of the sort, he would go for strength and comfort to the thirty-seventh Psalm. I have read it this morning to the young ladies with decided benefit to them and to myself." This note so greatly impressed me that I have never forgotten it, nor have I ever read the thirty-seventh Psalm without thinking of the dear woman and my happy life while near her.

The night we left Natchez to take the boat for Vicksburg, *en route* for Jackson, the Colonel had a great compliment paid him. The few men that were left of the military company and band that had been raised at Natchez for the Confederate army, marched up to the fort and escorted the Colonel's company to the boat amid cheers of the citizens. A great crowd had collected, and when the people on the boat learned the cause of the enthusiasm, our reception was slightly different from that at New Orleans; and I really feared from the numerous requests to ''have a drink with me,'' that there might be trouble for the Colonel later on, as he was usually the most abstemious man.

The journey to Vicksburg, which was about one hundred and twenty-five miles above Natchez, was delightful; the river was very high and much of the land was under water; travel on those magnificent boats was always a delight to me. There was so much of interest to be seen, and there were always charming people aboard. We made several trips during our stay South and they were always filled with interest. We reached the city safely and remained twenty-four hours. This city is also on a high bluff, and rises in terraces from the river. I wanted greatly to see where the great fighting had been done; where Farragut, in 1862, bombarded the place and passed the batteries with so little damage, and later when the invincible Grant with his forces succeeded in capturing the city and surrounding country. I rode on a fine horse with some officers, more than twenty miles over these battle-fields, where so many men on both sides gave up their lives. My own brother, only sixteen years old, had been with Grant's army at this place, which made this visit of more than usual interest.

Many of the officers and families stationed at Vicksburg had visited us at Natchez; among them were General Ord and his staff, General Gillem, who was colonel of our regiment, Captain Beach, who afterwards resigned and always regretted it, and many others. We were given a reception and dance, which I greatly enjoyed, not having had a dance since I left home, but I had plenty that night, for each officer considered it a duty, aside from the pleasure, to dance at least once with the guest. Here I again met Captain Gray, and I remember that I failed to relate a little incident that occurred before we left Natchez. One afternoon, just after dinner, Captain Gray came in to say "Good-bye;" he had gotten his promotion and was to go to another company. After sitting a little while he said, "Before I leave I have an apology I wish to make you."

I was rather surprised, as he had always been very polite. He continued, "You may remember I called on you at the hotel when you first arrived." I did. He said, "I returned to the garrison and said to these

42

officers (pointing to Lieutenants Churchill and Wesendorf), that I was sure we had caught a 'Tartar' from your very sharp nose. I now want to apologise to you, not only for saying it, but thinking it, and only wish I could serve the rest of my military life in the same garrison with you.'' We all laughed at the joke on me and tried to put him at his ease, for he seemed most uncomfortable. I had never known him very well; indeed he rarely went around with the other officers. He too, poor fellow, is dead.

CHAPTER III.

We left Vicksburg by rail for Jackson, where we arrived in the afternoon. We went to the hotel for a few days, until we could look at our "quarters" and get them in order. We found we were to have a very nice house in a beautiful garden, adjoining the garrison, which was quite large, both cavalry and infantry being there, and the Colonel was to be in command. The house was soon gotten in order; a little more furniture bought, pictures and curtains hung, piano rented, and new cases for books. In a week's time we were in order, and ready for the officers to come in to dinner or any meal, for during the Colonel's entire military life he kept open house. We received a very warm welcome on our arrival, both from the garrison and the citizens, letters having been written from Natchez to the gentlemen and their families introducing us.

The reconstruction of the States was going on and there was some unpleasant business there to be performed. A good deal of uneasiness had been felt in regard to turning the State over to the military, and the Colonel had been sent to see this successfully

44

Adelbert Ames

carried out with as little friction as possible, as he had shown his adaptability in getting along with the reconstruction in all of the Southern cities where he had been stationed. The civil officers were mostly Confederate soldiers and determined men. General Ames, the lieutenant-colonel of our regiment, whom the Government had appointed Military Governor, had called on the Colonel to put him in possession of the State House, as the Civil Governor had declined to give up the office. It was fortunate for the Colonel that most of the civil officers had been soldiers, for they realized the difficulty of his position. Of course it required great delicacy to gain the point without trouble. The Colonel took a sergeant and three men (though he had been advised to take a troop); the soldiers were left outside the State House. On going in he found the governor, some State officials, and a few of their friends. He bowed and told them he was called upon to perform a most unpleasant duty, but he would do it in the kindest manner he could, and would not attempt to expel them; he would simply place a sentinel at the door with instructions to allow all to pass out, but after they had passed out, none could return, or the sentinel would resist them. This made them the aggressors, if they attempted to return, as they would defy the power of the United States Government. All went well. They went out one by one; the last to leave was Governor Humphries, a fine, soldierly man, who understood the matter and felt the Colonel had done his duty as kindly and considerately as he could.

As I have said, reconstruction was taking place all over the South. When the States seceded they went out of the Union as far as they could; they withdrew their Representatives from Congress, and repudiated the laws of the United States; in the words of the South, "They seceded." At the end of the Civil War, or War of the States, the Government of the United States reasserted its authority, and Andrew Johnson, who became President of the United States (by reason of the assassination of that great man, President Lincoln), reorganised the establishment of the State government through the action of the white people alone. Congress refused to recognise the President's action, and held that the negro, being made free by the war, could find his protection in the ballot, as does the white man; with this object in view, Congress passed laws directing elections to be had throughout the seceded States under the control and direction of officers of the army. At these elections the whites and blacks were equally permitted to vote, electing all civil State officers from the highest to the lowest. The States thus reconstructed were admitted into the Union. I have always felt a pride that the State of Mississippi, of which we grew so fond, was so fortunate at this time in its governors (Ames and Alcorn) that the expenses incidental to the repairing and rebuilding public buildings and establishment of innumerable schools left the State in debt less than a half million dollars (as can be seen by the official records), a record made by few, if any, Northern States.

During the reconstruction, General Porter and General Babcock, two distinguished officers of General Grant's staff, came on a visit of inspection to Jackson. It was a great pleasure to meet these gentlemen, and we arranged a dinner for them by borrowing from the ladies in the garrison enough silver, glass and china, for the supply of each in those days was limited. Most of the officers on duty there were invited, among them being General Ames, Colonel Crane, Captain Sumner, Major Norton and Lieutenants Churchill and Corey. I was the only lady present as the scarcity of china would not permit of the others being asked; but they came and helped me arrange the table and to do many other necessary things, and joined us afterwards.

The dinner was very gay; and what gave great amusement to these men from the delightful city of Washington was that Jack, who with Dave had been left to take care of himself (while Caroline, their nurse, assisted the waiter), put his head in the dining-room door just as the man was bringing in an omelette soufflé and shouted: "Oh, Dave, they've got pudding!"

General Babcock died not long after this; but General Porter still lives and each year adds new laurels to his already brilliant record, the last being his interest in finding the body of Paul Jones, who did so much for the cause of liberty when our young country was going through its great struggle.

As I have said, General Ames, who had been appointed Military Governor, was also the lieutenant-colonel of our regiment (Eleventh Infantry). He was a young man of fine ability and had greatly distinguished himself during the war in several battles, besides being quite the hero of Fort Fisher. All of the civil offices were filled by army officers, and it was shortly after the installation of the Military Governor that Colonel Crane, who had been appointed mayor of the city of Jackson, was murdered by a man named Yerger, who had always held a good position in society and was well connected. Yerger, seeing Colonel Crane on the street, unbuttoned his cuffs and took them off, saying "he had some work to do." He coolly walked up to the Colonel and stabbed him to the heart. Yerger was immediately arrested by the soldiers and we expected a trial by court-martial, but

48

for some reason, although the city was under military rule, he was, some time later, turned over to the civil authorities and through some technicality of the law was released on bail. He removed to Baltimore (as public sentiment was so greatly against him in Jackson), where he dropped dead in the street some two years later. Every one was deeply grieved at this murder as Colonel Crane had been a great favorite with all of the better class of citizens as well as with the army. He was from Dayton, Ohio, a fine soldier, and a handsome, genial man, standing six feet two inches tall, and full of humor. I remember meeting him one morning and asking if he were going to the "hop" that night. "Oh, yes," he said, "I am going to see you dance, for I know if the floor were covered with eggs and you danced over them, not one would be broken." Another time he said to Mrs. Sumner, "I cannot understand how frail women like you and Ellen, who look as if a gentle wind would blow you over, can dance as you do; why you seem to possess more endurance than a government mule." There was, and is, a "hop" or informal dance every Friday evening in most army garrisons, especially those of the frontier; there is usually a good orchestra and army officers are proverbially good dancers. Besides, these gatherings bring the officers' families together and are generally delightful. An army woman usually keeps her youth because she dances so much; she rarely gives it up until her husband retires from service, and aside from the pleasure it is a most healthful exercise. I recall walking with Colonel Crane one morning across the garrison, when we were joined by General Ames and Major Norton. We came to a wide puddle of water (it had rained the night before); as quick as thought Colonel Crane seized the military cape from Major Norton's shoulders and threw it across the puddle, and taking my hand led me across, saying as we went, "Sir Walter Raleigh outdone."

The garrison life was most delightful; there were two troops of the Fifth Cavalry, and two companies of the Eleventh Infantry. The drills and parades were most interesting; the sound of the trumpets, and the band playing for guard mount, and other times during the day, was very inspiring; the officers dropping in informally during the day and evening always so cheerful and bright, and with their pretty speeches, made a halo around it all, and what a blessing it was so, for there were plenty of hardships to come for us all.

Jackson was the capital of the State; it was not so beautiful a city as Natchez, dear Natchez, always so dear to my heart, but the drives were beautiful and I rode horseback every day, generally with one of the lieutenants in the morning, when the Colonel was busy with his military duties, for he had much to do here. I remember with pleasure one young officer I rode often with, Galbraith Perry Rodgers, who sat his horse like a centaur, and rode magnificently. He was a dashing young cavalryman, over six feet tall and of splendid physique, with a good strong face. Alas! poor fellow, he died young, and had so much to live for. Then there was Captain Dwyer, who rode well, and had such a sympathetic voice; we made him sing for us always; and the clever Alfred Bache, always so charming and bright; and our dear Churchill—dead, all of them gone, splendid fellows all. Then there was Captain Charlie Wykoff (who, as I have mentioned, was afterwards killed at San Juan Hill, Cuba); and Captain Sam Sumner, another dashing young cavalryman, and his dear little wife, of whom I was always so fond; also her mother, Mrs. Bennett; Captain Wilson of the Fifth, who was always immaculately dressed; and Major Tom Norton, who was so big and good-natured, and so absent-minded that the officers used to make him believe he had had his breakfast when he had not. Then there were Lieutenant and Mrs. Lott; she was a very handsome young woman from Kentucky; also a very good-looking young lieutenant named Corey in Major Norton's company.

We were all so happy and light-hearted. The officers attended to their duties and then we were all together, riding, driving or walking; the outdoor life was so delightful. The evenings were spent with music, singing negro melodies or old songs that every one knew; usually some of the officers had a game of cards, and at about 9.30 we would have a little chafing-dish supper and then separate. One night in the week, usually Friday, we had a "hop" at the Governor's Mansion, General Ames being the Military Governor, and then the Fifth Cavalry Band, or part of it, played for us. Now, after so many years have passed, when I hear a strain of the beautiful "Blue Danube" or other Strauss waltzes, played so much at that time and to which I so often danced, I am thrilled through and through and carried back to the dear delightful days of my youth.

Sometimes we would take little trips to Vicksburg or other places in the State, where the Colonel would go on reconstruction business. They were always enjoyable, but I was glad to get back to the dear little home and my garden of roses and other choice plants we did not have in the North, and to the dear friends who welcomed me so heartily.

I remember so well going to New Orleans on a little visit,—Captain Sumner (now a major-general) and his wife, Mrs. Bennett, General Ames, the Colonel

LIEUTENANT GALBRAITH ROGERS, U.S.A.

MAJOR-GENERAL S. S. SUMNER, U.S.A.

and myself.[1] We went for the Mardi Gras and stopped at the famous old "Saint Charles Hotel." Not long ago I happened to be again in New Orleans. I walked over the Saint Charles as if in a dream. Nothing was familiar; I could recall no scene or place of the picture that had dwelt in my mind so many

---

[1] And here I feel I must say something more of that distinguished officer General Sumner. When only a lad he served in the Civil War and was brevetted three different times for gallantry. After the Civil War was over he was again brevetted for great gallantry in action against Indians at Summit, Colorado. When the Spanish War came on he was colonel of the famous Sixth Cavalry. He took his regiment to Chickamauga, Tennessee, and was there appointed brigadier-general of volunteers, and assigned to command the First Cavalry Brigade, his brigade forming part of the expedition to San Diego, Cuba. He served through the entire campaign, after which he was appointed a major-general of volunteers for his distinguished services. After the war was over General Sumner was selected for service as military attaché at the Court of St. James. He remained in England until July, 1900, when at his own request he was relieved from duty and hastened to join his regiment in China. The services of the Sixth Cavalry are too well known for me to go into detail. After the war in China, where General Sumner had commanded a provisional brigade, he took his regiment to the Philippines, where he again did gallant work, and was appointed a brigadier-general of the regular army in 1901. He remained in the Philippines three years, and in 1903 was appointed a major-general.

years. Upon inquiry I found the old hotel with its charming environment had been destroyed; the one I was in had been erected on the same site; but the passing of the old house had not obliterated the memories that linger round it. (Pardon the digression, if digression it is.)

When we arrived we met Major McCall, an old Philadelphia friend of the Colonel, who had a plantation just above the city on the Mississippi River. He gave us a dinner at "The Belenger," the then famous restaurant, where we saw the wonderful procession of the "Mystic Crewe of Comus" from a balcony, after which we drove to the theatre to witness the ball. We had a box where we could see everything. My friend Mrs. Marston and the Major were with us, and Emma and I slipped out of the box to have a dance with two of the men in grand uniform —aides to the King of Comus. All too soon it was time for us to go home, and when we got to our carriage, we found our husbands were not going home with us; they were going to have a "peep" at the French Ball, while Major McCall would take us home. We begged for a "peep" also; but no, they were obdurate. After getting into the carriage we begged and implored the Major to take us. The poor man could not refuse, and finally said that if we would promise to go in a latticed box, where we could not be seen, he would take us for a few minutes. Of course, we promised; so we stopped at a costumer's and each got a domino and mask. When we got to Mrs. Shaw's to change our gowns, she tried in every way to persuade us not to go; but we, too, were obdurate, so she helped us dress and we were soon off.

When we reached the Opera House my heart began to beat wildly. All was new to me. I had been raised very carefully in a quiet little church-going town, and knew but little of the gay world, except what I had seen at my father's house. We got inside the foyer, when Mrs. Marston, who was born and raised in New Orleans, and had all the charm and culture of a young society woman, raised in that city and by such a distinguished mother, knew exactly what to do; and having full courage, taking my hand, said, "Come quickly!" and I, none the less willing, followed. In a moment we had left the Major in the crowd and were in the ball-room on the floor—and there happened a strange thing. The first man to approach us was the Colonel, who offered me his arm for a promenade. (The men were not masked, only the women.) We walked for a short distance, when he asked me to take his other arm, which I did, and in a moment he said: "Well, my dear, now that you have seen the ball-room, don't you think we had better go home?'' My astonishment can be better imagined than expressed.

However, we remained until midnight, dancing and talking with different men, some of whom we knew, and we puzzled them greatly. I was thrilled with the excitement of the scene, for it was the first ''Bal Masque'' I had ever seen. When we recovered from the astonishment of our husbands joining us, they told us that Mrs. Shaw had sent a note by a faithful coloured servant, to Major Marston, telling him that we would be there and for them to be on the lookout for us. She had not only described our dominos, but, fearing others might be there like them, had marked the right sleeve. She said she knew we would not remain in a latticed box when once we were inside of the Opera House. I have always been glad I saw the sight that night, as I have never seen anything like it since,—such wonderfully beautiful gowns of satin in all colours, and lace, marvellous lace to my eyes, and such dancing and high kicking! It was many years before the high kicking in dancing became the vogue here in the North, or the South either. I think I may say, I thoroughly enjoyed it all, and I may add that no one ever knew we were there but the men who looked after us, and this is the first time it has ever been told. There is much I would like to tell about the ball, but as this little reminiscence is for my grandchildren, perhaps I had better not.

I would like to say a word about the coloured servant man who carried the note to Major Marston. I was told that he had been a slave in Mr. Shaw's family for a number of years, and was their butler when the war broke out. Mr. Shaw, who was a Southern man, gave generously of his wealth to the Confederacy to help buy ships, ammunition, etc. When New Orleans fell into our hands, much property, silverware, jewels, etc., were confiscated. Mr. Shaw had died, but Mrs. Shaw's house was thoroughly searched a number of times without anything of value being found. This servant, who had remained faithful to the family, was repeatedly asked where the treasures were kept, but would never tell. He was finally imprisoned and kept some days, but he remained true to his mistress and never divulged where the things had been placed for safety.

One afternoon during this visit Captain and Mrs. Sumner, Mrs. Bennett and General Ames went for a drive to Lake Pontchartrain. I intended returning some calls, and the Colonel had gone to the races with friends. Just as I was ready to start who should arrive but Lieutenant Wesendorf from the garrison at Jackson. He had gotten a twenty-four hours' "leave" and ran down to see if we were all having a good time, and to see New Orleans. He was most anxious to see the French or Creole part of the town. Off we went. We crossed Canal Street, where the negroes sat with their bright-colored bandana handkerchiefs wrapped picturesquely round their heads, selling prelines; we were soon in the old French quarter. The architecture was entirely different; there were silent old houses with charming interior courtyards; the inhabitants seemed to be asleep, the whole place was so quiet. After a long walk over this romantic part of the town, we went into an old French confectioner's for some chocolate and sweets; it was delightfully clean, the floor covered with white sand, the linen spotless; there were pretty French prints on the wall, besides innumerable pictures of Napoleon, as will be seen in all restaurants. It was all very fascinating, and we lingered longer than we intended. When we started I was amazed to see the street-lamps lighted, and the shades of night fast falling; we hurried along, got an omnibus at Canal Street, which soon landed us at the hotel, but not before a great commotion had occurred. All were greatly alarmed at my absence. We met Captain Sumner on the pavement much excited, who told us that each one had gone to different places looking for me, and the Colonel had just decided to see the chief of police, as he was sure something must have hap-

pened to me. The reason of all this excitement was, that up to that time I had always lived in a garrison and was generally in the house at twilight; so that my absence in a large city after sundown, and alone, as they all supposed, had given some alarm. After the excitement cooled down and they saw Lieutenant Wesendorf, he was given a hearty welcome, although he was really the culprit, but I had had a most charming afternoon.

We returned to Jackson the following day, I completely tired out with the excitement of all I had seen and done; but the memory of that visit will ever remain with me. I afterward made a visit to Mrs. Marston, and had the pleasure of meeting and knowing General Sheridan, one of the greatest cavalry officers that ever lived; also knew his staff officers— Colonel Schuyler Crosby, who was then one of the handsomest men in the army; Dr. Morris Asche; the two Forsyths ("Tony" and "Sandy," as they were called); and General Sawtelle; all fine soldiers and agreeable men. What a gay visit it was! What delightful rides, drives, dinners and dances we had, and what flowers! I never smell the odour of violets without being carried back to those dear delightful days, when my room was filled with them.

It was only a short time after my return to Jackson from this visit that the order came for us to move to Texas. We had been here nearly two years and the thought had scarcely occurred to me that some day I must go. Indeed, I thought my heart would break to give up my dear little home, my garden and flowers, in which I had taken such interest, and the dear friends whom I had learned to love so dearly; besides I had such a horror of Texas, and I was not very well. But it had to be done. Things were packed ready to move, yet when the last moment came I could not go; the packing had been too much for me and the doctor said I must keep perfectly quiet in my bed for at least two weeks. The Colonel and the troops got off, and I, the children and nurse stayed with friends until I was able to take the journey. It was hard to say "Good-bye." My nature at that time was so intense I could not help loving the dear people who were so kind and made my life almost one great holiday, and whom I might never see again. Indeed, as I look back to that period of my life I can hardly understand the great joy that filled my heart; life seemed so real, friends so sincere, the days were filled with sunshine, and the air redolent with the odour of ever-blooming flowers. For the first time in my existence I realised the soul within me and that the world was beautiful to live in. Is it any wonder that I love the State of Mississippi, where I, too, unfolded as the flowers did, and developed from the girl into the woman? "O sweet past, sometimes remembrance raises thy long veil, then we weep in recognising thee!"

All too soon the day came for us to start,—my two little men, the good Caroline, and myself. We left in the afternoon, journeying over the same road which had given me so much pleasure only a short time before. I could not help crying, much to Jack's sorrow. It was an unusual sight to him and he put his arms around me and said: "Why do you cry, mámma?" and I said: "Oh, dear child, I don't want to go to Texas; it is so far off." (I did not realise that later I should go many, many miles further off, and without the dear boys who were my pride and delight.)

While Jack and I were talking, he trying to comfort me (as he has since done in all his life when trouble and distress came upon me), two gentlemen near, hearing our conversation, spoke to me and said Texas was not such a bad place, and gave me quite a bit of information about it, saying many of the rough element of the volunteer armies on both sides had been disbanded in Eastern Texas. They had become very lawless, and the Government was determined to put that element down at once; besides, the reconstruction was not going smoothly, so the regular troops were being ordered into the State—and I may say right here that order was restored within a few months after their arrival.

That night, after every one had retired, we were suddenly awakened by that awful and unmistakable sound of croup; poor Jack was in the throes. The men who had talked to me a few hours before were up in a moment to see what they could do. They first wet a towel and bound it round his throat and put a dry one over it; then they found some one on the train who had ipecac, which was given, and after a couple of hours of great anxiety the child fell asleep, and I realised that there were good people everywhere, even from Texas.

We reached New Orleans early in the morning, where we remained until the following day. I had no desire to go out or to see any one, though several kind friends came to see us. It seemed so different compared to the other times I had been in this gay city, and I dreaded to take the journey which was before me, alone. For the first time in my life my spirits had deserted me and I seemed to have a foreboding that all would not be well.

The next morning after our arrival in New Orleans we took the steamer to cross the Gulf of Mexico to Galveston, a most disagreeable journey. As we went on board, who should I see but the two men who had been so kind to us on the train; I really greeted them as old friends. Caroline was sick all the way over; fortunately, I was a good sailor, for I had two pretty active lads to look after. We parted with our fellow passengers at Galveston. The Colonel, who met me, thanked them for their courtesy and kindness, and I said "Good-bye," forgetting we might never meet again, and I have always regretted that I did not know the names of the two men to whom I was so grateful.

We went to the hotel for a night's rest and continued our journey the next day. We took the cars and rode several hours to the terminus of the road, and there took a comfortable ambulance with four good mules for the rest of the journey.

CHAPTER IV.

I DO not remember much about Galveston, but the thing that made the greatest impression about the place was the fact that everything we owned was ruined there. The trunks and boxes had been left out in a three days' rain on the wharf. The Colonel had been obliged to push on with the troops, the luggage to come after. Somehow ours was left; who was to blame I never knew. It was not only our clothes, but the household linen, kitchen things, and indeed, as I have said before, everything. I especially grieved over a new gray silk gown that I had not worn, and a gray silk hat with pink roses, which had been the delight of my heart, but Caroline said: "Oh! Missus, I never did think you looked so pretty in that thar hat, as you do in the one you's wearin'." I knew she said it to help comfort me and I cheered up a bit.

The ride to Brenham was pleasant. It was the first of my long frontier rides. The command was in tents about a mile from the town. The Colonel, knowing I would not be able to live in that way, had hired, furnished, the half of a house occupied and owned by a gentleman and his wife, named Diller, from Pennsylvania. For several days I had no cook. The Colonel got up in the morning, made the fire and put on the kettle with water, Caroline dressed the boys, set the table and went into the kitchen to assist. Fortunately, we never cared for a hearty breakfast; soon a pot of good coffee was made, bacon fried crisp, and eggs were boiled; the only thing not good was the bread, so I decided that I must make it. And here, for the first time, my lessons in cooking really came into service; for even after I got a cook, I made the bread. The Colonel would carry the lamp, and he and I would go into the kitchen after the cook had gone home for the night; I would set the sponge, or if it had been set, I would make out the rolls for breakfast and put them in the pan, and it was easy for Caroline to spread a little sweet milk over them in the morning (with a clean piece of linen) and put them in the oven. I always made enough to send a loaf or two up to the camp for the ladies and children.

The life at Brenham was hard in every way; murders were committed constantly; the Colonel had charge of six counties, and there was scarcely a day that he was not called upon by the authorities of the town to send out men to arrest desperadoes. You may have some idea of the condition of things from

the following: One day I went on the porch to see
where the lads were. I saw Jack lying flat on the
ground with arms extended, and Dave with a long
stick, aiming at him. I quickly called: "What are
you doing?" "Oh, nothing," Jack replied; "we are
playing. I am a dead man; Dave has just shot me."
I decided then and there that it was not the atmosphere in which to bring up boys, and determined to
take them as soon as possible to their grandparents.

As I have said, the whole command was in tents.
The poor ladies had a terrible time; many of them
were delicately bred, and they had all of their own
work to do, often washing and ironing. The lieutenants could not afford to pay house-rent for their
families, and servants' wages were exorbitantly high,
and there were very few to be had at any price, as
most of the negroes had gone north. It was very
lonely for me. The Colonel, being in command, left
the house early in the morning, came back at about
two o'clock for a hurried dinner, and returned to
the post until after retreat. Often he was called out
at night by the town authorities to quell some dis-
turbance or arrest murderers. I was in a very delicate
condition of health, and night after night when the
Colonel would be obliged to go out I would get up,
as I could not sleep, wrap a shawl round me and sit
in a corner on the floor near the window, where I

could watch if any one came in the gate. The windows had no shades nor outside shutters, only a thin muslin curtain; there was nothing else to be had; and I was dreadfully afraid lest some of those terrible creatures would come in to rob and kill us, knowing the Colonel was away. In consequence my nerves got into a frightful condition, but although I was ill, I kept up. The Colonel had so much to attend to, the condition of affairs being so dreadful, that I hated to add trouble to his mind about the real condition of my health. One of our officers, Captain Haller, who had been promoted from the ranks of a New York regiment for great gallantry in planting our colours twice, after they had been shot down, was brutally murdered, when he had gone out to make an arrest, and his body was not discovered for months after. The Colonel would often go out at night to make an arrest without taking a guard with him, so I was constantly anxious lest his life would be taken.

We had some bright days, and then I would take the boys and go out to the camp for a walk, or would drive. The Colonel had gotten me a nice comfortable carriage from Galveston, and the afternoon drive with the children was the pleasantest time of the day. One afternoon when the carriage drove up I noticed a strange driver, and on inquiry found that my own man was not well. I did not like the looks or manner of this man, but got in the carriage with the children and we were soon in the country. I must say for Texas that I have never seen in any State or Territory such quantities of wild flowers of all colours and wonderfully beautiful; great fields of them as far as the eye could reach. There was an especially beautiful red flower which grew in great abundance. If memory serves me right it was called "flag" or Iris. My little lads used to go almost crazy over these carpets of lovely flowers when we went to gather them. The thousands of cattle we would see grazing were also interesting, and the sunsets were glorious with the gold and purple lights. The roads were good and, as I have said, it was a pleasure to drive.

On the afternoon I mentioned we had gotten well out into the country when I saw our driver was so drunk he was in danger of falling from the carriage, and the horses were greatly excited. As soon as I realized our danger, I told the boys to lie flat on the bottom of the carriage, and notwithstanding the horses were now running, I succeeded in climbing through the window into the seat next the driver and took the reins from him. Although I could not stop the horses at once I guided them; fortunately the road was broad, and there were but few teams on it. No one came to our rescue, but after the horses had run some distance we came to a cross road, into which I turned them, thinking it would take us nearer home, which it did. Gradually the horses stopped running; poor things, they were not vicious, only frightened and excited from the man pulling them. As soon as they heard my voice they quieted down but trembled all over with fear. When we got in sight of our cottage I saw the Colonel on the sidewalk talking with Captain Whitney. I drove up to the house and he took in the situation at once and took the horses' heads; I remember no more about it for I had fainted, the relief being so great. Colonel carried me into the house, while the boys jumped from the bottom of the carriage and told what had happened. Captain Whitney took the horses to the stable to see that they had proper treatment, while the driver was sent to the guard-house to sober up and reap the consequences. I often wondered where I got the strength to guide the horses as I did.

We made no friends or acquaintances at Brenham; every one stood aloof from the "Yankees," though they wanted us for their protection, and I think I may say that no life was safe at that time without the regular troops being in the vicinity.

Our good friends the Dillers were exceptions. I shall never forget them, for I should not have lived had it not been for their kindness. We had no pleasure, except the afternoon drive when I was able to

go, my books had all been destroyed with the other
things and there were none to be had in the town,
so the days hung heavily. Soon, however, something
occurred that demanded all of my time: poor Jack
was poisoned by the poisonous oak that grew in
abundance (as I learned later). The lad had begged
to be allowed to go in his bare feet, as the other children did, and I, thinking it would be good for him,
allowed it, with terrible result. As soon as we discovered the rash we sent for the army doctor, and
later for the resident physician, thinking he might
know more about the poisons in his own locality, but
neither helped him; the poison entered his whole sys-
tem and he became so emaciated we carried him on a
pillow for weeks. The treatment, too, seemed to me
heroic and I fainted every day when the doctor came to
dress the little feet, knowing what the child suffered.
As the spring advanced the weather became hot and
changeable; ofttimes I would put on a thin linen
gown and go on the porch hoping to catch a breath
of air, and suddenly the wind would rise without the
least warning and would blow almost a cyclone and
the thermometer would drop forty degrees.

The nervous strain I was under, besides the trying
climate, was fast telling on me, and the doctor insisted
upon my going North, especially as the command was
shortly to march to Fort Griffen, and although that

was a more healthful place, he feared I would not stand the fatigue of the journey. After we decided it was best for the boys and me to go to my parents for the summer, it did not take long to get off. There were no household goods to be packed, only the few things we had saved from the destruction of our luggage. I think I was never so glad to leave any place; even the most remote frontier garrison I have ever been in held more attractions than Brenham at that time, but I am told it is now a delightful city; still, I have no wish to see it. The memory of all my mental and physical sufferings there can never be obliterated. The Colonel got a few days' leave and took us to Galveston, put us on the boat and in the captain's charge, who looked after us and kindly took us to the St. Charles Hotel, at New Orleans, where friends soon came to us, and where we remained for a few days' visit; the sea had been fairly smooth and none of us were seasick. We got a comfortable drawing-room on the cars and at Jackson, Mississippi, much to our surprise and delight some old friends got on the train. A funny little incident occurred just after we left New Orleans. When we reached Galveston I noticed that Dave had a little rash on his face, and sent for the doctor to examine him well as I feared he might be getting measles or chicken-pox. Unfortunately we spoke of it in the child's

71

presence. After carefully watching him the doctor decided that the rash was caused by eating sweets, so we kept on our journey. Soon after leaving New Orleans Dave climbed up, stood on the seat, and announced to the passengers: "We think I am getting the measles, but maybe it is the chicken-pox." The gentleman sitting immediately in front of him jumped up and left the car, and the others were much alarmed. I begged Caroline to assure the people it was not so, but the rash on his face looked suspicious and all gave us a wide berth, much to my amusement.

We made the journey in a fairly comfortable way, I lying down most of the time, while my friends did everything possible for me.

At Louisville, Kentucky, we stopped for a short rest at the Galt House. The dining-room was very beautiful, with large mirrors set in the walls, and fine chandeliers of cut glass, which made the room very brilliant when lighted. My little lads had never seen such a dazzling sight, and when we reached the dining-room door that evening, Dave, who was a magnificent looking child, gave a whoop of delight, ran down the center of the room, and stood on his head. I scarcely knew what to do, but the head waiter gave Jack and me seats and then went after Dave, who had already been captured and was being brought to me on the shoulder of a gentleman, to the amusement of every one.

We finally reached Philadelphia in safety. My father was at that time stationed in Baltimore, but the weather was getting warm and he felt I needed a more bracing air and had taken a house in Delaware County, Pennsylvania, on high ground and near a most excellent physician, Doctor Garretson.

For weeks after reaching my parents' home I was desperately ill, and really had no idea that I should live. The terrible climate of that little frontier town, and the anxieties and cares there endured by me, had undermined an excellent constitution; however, with watchful care and good nursing, I gradually, slowly but surely, got stronger, and experienced the great joy of having a daughter born to us the following autumn—Ellen.

The child, as may be imagined after all that I had gone through, was very fragile; and when but a few months old she became desperately ill with some enteric fever and we surely would have lost her had it not been for the devoted care and good nursing of her father, who was then "on leave." He allowed no one to do anything for her but himself. He had a sailor's hammock swung on the wide gallery that encircled the house, and he kept her there day and night, always in the fresh air. He slept when she slept and, indeed, scarcely left her unless she were sleeping, and the child was saved to us.

When we were both stronger the Colonel took us to Long Branch, which was then the fashionable resort. The sea air soon made us both strong, and we greatly enjoyed our stay at the "West End," where we met some old friends, and made new ones. We were there a month. I then took the baby home and left her with the boys and nurse with my dear mother, while my husband and I went to Saratoga for the races, of which he was very fond, and although it was the first time in my life that I had seen races I enjoyed them greatly, and have always gone since when opportunity offered. The Colonel was very lucky that year in picking the winners; he had always had horses and was a good judge of them.

On our return from Saratoga we stopped at the old "New York Hotel," corner of Broadway and Fourth Street, where we met many of our old friends from Natchez and New Orleans, Mr. John Minor and family being among the number; also Mr. Alfred Davis, whom the Colonel was delighted to see and I none the less pleased. What pleasure it was to talk over the delightful days spent in Natchez, and to go on little shopping excursions in the morning and drives to the park in the afternoon!

Generally, we went to the theatre or a concert at

LIEUTENANT JOHN LAWRENCE CHURCHILL, U.S.A.

night, our husbands usually leaving us at the hotel door on our return, while they went to the club. I remember one night the Colonel came in and I awakened and said: "Why, isn't it late?" "A quarter of twelve," he answered. I pulled out my watch, looked at it and said: "Something has happened to my watch; it is three o'clock." I soon fell asleep, but the next day on going out I left the watch at the jewelry store to be repaired, and the following day asked the Colonel to stop for it and bring it to me. He was greatly surprised and asked why I took it there (the watch was comparatively new). "Don't you remember," I replied, "it had stopped the other night when you came in? You said it was a quarter of twelve and my watch had stopped at three in the afternoon." The Colonel roared. "Well," he said, "three is a quarter of twelve, isn't it?" I saw the joke he had played on me, but I was even, as he had two dollars and a half to pay for repairs and cleaning the watch, which I must add never kept as good time afterward.

I also had the pleasure at this time of visiting Lieutenant Churchill's family in New York and talking with them about their brother and seeing a fine portrait of him. Mr. Churchill was a gentleman of the old school, dignified and courteous, with great charm of manner, and there was a strong resemblance between father and son. I had a most delightful visit. I remember one evening we were dressed to go to a promenade concert. Miss Anna went into her father's room at the last moment and took the glass shade from the gas, and forgetting a moment pushed back the bracket; the lace curtains immediately took fire. The wood work was all of oiled walnut, and the ceiling was exquisitely frescoed in oils. The fire soon extended and was frightful. The girls were terrified and begged me to tell the maids and men what to do. The engines and crowd were at the door insisting upon coming in, but we would not allow any one to enter. I pinned up my violet silk gown and we all worked harder than we ever had done in our lives. I never saw such willing service given by maids and men carrying buckets of water and fighting the flames. Finally we got the fire out and three more exhausted or frightened young women would have been hard to find; however, we recovered and went to the concert. The next day Mr. Churchill returned from his visit up the Hudson, where he had been visiting his daughter Mrs. Satterlee (the wife of the present Bishop of Washington); he went to his room and saw the ruin of what had before been so beautiful. While the girls were telling him about the fire, and regretting it, he stopped them and taking them in his arms said, ''This is nothing; let us

be thankful your lives were saved and no one hurt.''
Of course he won my heart. Each day of my visit
with Mr. Churchill's family I was impressed with the
great calamity that had befallen not only them but
society at large, in that the son of such a man had
to give up his life, dying in the South of fever. True,
he died while serving his country, but it has always
seemed to me a terrible tragedy, knowing how those
dear fellows lived, often in tents on low or marshy
ground. It is sad to look back to those days and
realise how many have passed beyond.

We returned to my father's home for a few weeks.
The time sped all too quickly; the Colonel's ''leave''
was up; he was to join his regiment, the First Cavalry
(to which he had been transferred), at Benecia, California.

I was to go to New York with him for a few last
days and then to return to my parents. It was considered best for him to go out alone, and find out
just where he was to be stationed permanently, and
get the quarters in order before I and the little family should join him. When we were on the boat crossing the ferry to New York a man came to the Colonel
and asked to see his trunk checks. When they were
shown he coolly said that my trunk had been knocked
from the luggage-crate into the river; it had been recovered but the grappling irons had broken it and

the top tray with contents had been lost. All of my
jewelry (save the few rings and pin I had on) and
my laces which the Colonel's mother had given me
(and were priceless) were gone, and the balance of
the things in the trunk, including the baby's layette,
were ruined almost beyond repair as may be imagined,
the trunk being broken open at the bottom of the river.
Thus in a short time I had two great trials of
patience. Perhaps I should say the railroad officials
immediately offered me six hundred dollars which I
took, as I was in no condition of health to bring suit
for heavier damages, and the Colonel was joining his
regiment without delay.

I remained with my parents some months, growing
stronger every day and better fitted for the frontier
life that was before me. The Colonel staid but a few
months at Benecia Barracks, California, and was
then ordered to Camp Halleck, Nevada. Although
the post was very isolated it was considered healthful,
so again we packed our little belongings and started
on our journey, which was then considered long and
fatiguing, occupying seven days from New York to
San Francisco. Our little daughter drank milk from
a bottle, and the difficulty seemed to be, keeping the
milk sweet for many hours. There were no dining-
cars or cold storage in those days, only the primitive
sleepers, which have been so greatly improved since.

78

My mother went to a tinsmith and had a small refrigerator made, about fifteen inches long, ten wide and eight high. It was complete; had handles and a double bottom, which fitted on the outside and caught the water that came from the piece of ice within. I may say right here that we never had any trouble; we were able to get fresh milk where we got our meals, and never once did the milk become sour over night on our journey. I had secured a most excellent but very plain Irish nurse about thirty years old, who had charge of the baby. Her name was Bridget, and I shall no doubt allude to her often hereafter, as she was with me eight years or thereabout.

We started from Philadelphia. My little lads were now quite self-reliant and hearty, and were no trouble whatever. Their lives had been so different from those of city children that they were quite interesting to our fellow-travellers. When we got off the train three times a day for our meals, some of the gentlemen would take them along by the hand, and at every stop of five minutes along the route they would be jumped off the train to have a good run; so they kept well the entire journey.

CHAPTER V.

WE reached Halleck station in the evening at about seven o'clock. The Colonel met us. Our luggage was soon put on an army wagon and we were comfortably settled in the ambulance drawn by four mules, when the Colonel said: "All set, Price." The mules started on a gallop, which considerably startled me, until the Colonel reassured me by telling me that the Pacific Coast mules always ran and did not trot, as the Eastern mules did. I suppose they, too, imbibed the spirit of the country at that date.

The garrison was thirteen miles from the station, up in the foothills of the Humboldt Mountains. We were glad to reach the little home. The commanding officer's house being occupied, the Colonel took a smaller set of quarters; but they were quite comfortable and better than I had had at either Macon or on my first arrival at Natchez; they were built of adobe, with a hall in the center and two rooms on each side, each twelve feet square. Outside, the back porch had been enclosed, which we used for a dining-room; the kitchen was separate from the house, and we had an excellent Chinaman cook, named Joe. We

also had a nice wide porch in the front of the house.
The morning after our arrival I went on the porch
to look at our surroundings. I found the mountains
—great rugged peaks—around three sides of us; the
country in front of us was a gradual descent to the
station, and beyond high mountains rose in the distance. Many times afterwards I stood on the porch
and saw the trains passing thirteen miles distant, the
atmosphere was so clear.

The officers' quarters were well back, in a straight
line against the foothills; facing the parade-ground,
on the right, were the adjutant's office, the commissary and quartermaster's buildings; on the left were
the long low quarters for the men; at the end, also
facing the officers' quarters, were the stables, leaving
a square for parade-ground of about five hundred
feet. Running just by the side of our house was a
most beautiful clear mountain stream. I could hear
the sound of the water as it dashed over the stones
from my window. Often the Colonel would take his
rod and flies and catch a basket of delicious trout
for our breakfast. Game of all kinds was to be found
in the vicinity and after the Colonel's morning duties
were over he would jump into his shooting clothes
and go off, often walking twenty-five miles, and bring
back from ten to fifty birds, ducks, grouse, quail,
prairie-chickens and sage-hens; he would always draw

the latter as soon as killed so there was no taste of sage left in the bird. He kept the garrison supplied with game, for he was the best shot in the Department and it always remained his pride to be so in every Department in which he was stationed. I often went shooting with him. We would take the boys and drive out to a stream and spend the day in the open. The Colonel would go off down the stream and the boys would take the seats from the ambulance and make us comfortable in the shade of the willows. By the time their lessons were said it would be noon. I would then make the coffee, the driver, Price, and the lads making the fire and bringing the water. Soon we would hear a shot and know the master was coming. He would broil some quail or a teal duck and we would have a luncheon fit for a king. I was never afraid of the Indians in this locality, they always seemed so peaceful and quiet, though troops were stationed at Camp Halleck for the protection of the settlers and the railroad. After our luncheon was over the Colonel would go off shooting down the other side of the stream; we would follow slowly in the ambulance until he was ready to return. The birds would be taken from his pockets (much to the delight of the boys, who were fast becoming young sportsmen), put on the floor of the ambulance, and home we would drive. It was at Camp Halleck I first

learned to sew. I had to make all the clothes my
children and I wore, besides the household linen. It
was a very difficult task for me to make the little
trousers that my lads now wore, especially putting in
the pockets, and I tried very hard to buy them off,
but they were never willing to give them up; they
would stand, one each side of me, helping to get
them in right.

As I have said, I was never afraid of these Indians.
The Shoshones and Pah Utes often came into the
house and brought skins, beaver and otter, also
baskets and bead-work, for sale; we always bought
some little thing from them. I often wish now that
I had some of the beautiful skins I then used for
rugs. I think I have but two things left which we
got there—one, a large Indian basket, used for thirty
years and still as good as ever, and some old fur.

I rode every day, and here it was that I came near
having a bad accident, which I have already mentioned. A man driving a drove of horses up from
Texas stopped at the fort. He had some fine-looking
horses, one a beautiful sorrel mare that I wanted very
much. I mounted her, found she was well gaited, and
seemed as gentle as a kitten; I rode her all around
the garrison and the officers and ladies who rode came
out to admire her. I was so pleased with her the
Colonel bought her for me. For three days after the

purchase it rained, so all I could do was to go to the stable and see the pretty creature. When the sun came out, I sent for the mare to be saddled, but the sergeant in charge of the stables asked the Colonel's permission to go with us as he did not like the mare's actions. Colonel ordered his horse, and his orderly also to go with us. The horses were brought up and I gaily tripped down the steps and mounted. Fortunately for me, both the Colonel and sergeant stood by her head; she threw herself back on her haunches, standing almost straight, then plunging forward and then back, striking me with her head; the sergeant made a spring and caught her, but she broke away twice. The Colonel insisted upon my jumping off, but it was almost impossible. Several soldiers had run up to my rescue, and finally, after they got her head firmly, I jumped and the Colonel caught me. The trouble was, she had been over-fed in the stable; she had had no exercise, and during the long march from Texas she had had no grain whatever. The next day I went down to the stable to see her, and perhaps take a ride; what was my consternation and vexation to find her gone. Colonel had sold her to a ranchman for almost nothing, fearing I might try again to ride her. The sergeant insisted she was crazy, a statement I never quite believed.

One Fourth of July morning I went with a party
of young officers and ladies to ride to the top of one
of the mountains. We rode on a trail through a most
beautiful cañon. It was so silent and peaceful, there
was not a sound to be heard but the ripple of the
little stream as it came from the mountain; in some
places the ascent was very steep, and the brush and
young pines were constantly in our way; but we
were all anxious to get to the top and see the view
of the other valley. We had taken a good luncheon
with us, which we ate about noon, when the horses
were given a little feed that we had carried with us.
After a short rest we started on again, the weather
getting very cold, still we pushed on until, suddenly
making a turn, we found we had reached the snow—
and what a scene met our eyes! The view extended
for miles. All around us were huge granite mountains and great looming peaks that were covered with
snow, while far as the eye could reach was the great
sage-brush desert, a scene of silence and desolation.
We were well rewarded for our climb, and would
like to have gone further on, but the snow was so
deep we found it to be impossible. One of the men
put some of it in a feed bag for us to carry back with
us, fearing our story might be doubted.

We found the descent very difficult, the trail being
very narrow, and it was harder to push aside the

brush going down than it had been in going up; besides, the precipice on our right seemed deeper and more threatening. Indeed, it was with a sigh of relief that we reached the desert valley again.

And I doubt if any of us who are living have forgotten the day, or the still picture we saw from the snow-clad mountain top.

One evening, after dinner, Lieutenant Bacon came in hurriedly, saying the quartermaster sergeant had deserted, taking the money from the safe, and that he with a couple of men would have to go after him, as he had been seen going in the direction of Elko, the nearest town, thirty miles distant. The Colonel and other officers had gone to "Fort Winnemucca" for a few days on court-martial duty. Lieutenant Bacon asked if I would be afraid to remain in the camp without an officer. I was not, but told him he had better send Lieutenant Cresson's wife to stay with me, as she might be afraid, not having had any frontier experience. Off the men went, Mrs. Cresson and I getting our rifles ready, in case they should be needed, and which we knew how to handle; for all the ladies in those days went out to target practice and were taught the use of firearms.

We will not follow Lieutenant Bacon, but I will say, they caught the man, shots were exchanged, the sergeant was killed and the money regained after

a very exciting night ride over the sage brush. This
upset my household completely as Bridget, in spite of
having no beauty, was engaged to be married to the
sergeant. She had given him her savings—over three
hundred dollars—and had told us nothing about it,
as he had asked her not to mention it. Poor Bridget!
I think she grieved after the rascally sergeant much
more than she did for her money.

We had some pleasant people at this post: Col.
Ned Baker, son of the gallant General Baker of
Oregon, and his charming wife from Tennessee; he
was one of the most generous, big-hearted men I ever
knew; everyone was fond of him, and his death, some
years later, was universally regretted; Captain Thompson and wife, Captain Stacy and family, and Lieutenant Palmer Wood and his pretty wife and cherub
children. Most of the girls grew to be beautiful
women and married in the army; two of them have
died, and the two young sons, who were gallant and
brave, gave up their lives in the service of their
country. One died in Cuba and the other was killed
in the Philippines. Years after we left Halleck I
met Captain and Mrs. Wood with great pleasure in
Arizona. She was still very beautiful, and the great
grief that was to come upon her had not yet entered
her life.

We often had visits from the officers stationed in

San Francisco; they would come on duty of one kind
or another. It was always a delight to us to see them,
as they brought us news from the outside world.

I remember a visit from General French, of the
artillery, who was in command at the "Presidio."
He was a most gallant officer and had commanded a
corps in the Army of the Potomac during the war.
He was also a charming talker, and I have been told
that after the war was over no dinner in Washington
was complete without him. He, too, died many years
ago. We also had a visit from Colonel Ramsey,
another delightful man with a fine war record.
Afterward when he was stationed in Washington he
was said to be President Arthur's double. General
Willcox, Major Thornberg (who was afterwards killed
at the hand of the Utes), Major Throckmorton, Lieutenant Schenck, and many others visited us, and last,
but not least, came that great soldier General Schofield. Of course he came on duty, but my pride was
very great at having him as a guest at our little house.
The Colonel had served a long time under his command during the war and knew him well, but,
although I had never met him, he soon seemed like
an old friend. His manner was simple, and in the
pleasure of talking with him I completely forgot our
ugly little room of twelve feet square with its white-
washed walls and ugly reddish paint. It seemed to

me while in the army, that the quartermasters were always using up scraps of paint; no two rooms were alike and each one uglier than the other. It was only a few months after the visit of the General that his friendship for us was proven, for through his great kindness in sending a special doctor to me my life was saved.

Had it not been for these occasional visits, life would have been very dreary. Camp Halleck was but a two-company post; there was nothing, but an occasional ride over the sage-brush plains, to relieve the monotony of our life; had it not been for my children, my two boys in particular, who were hearty and thoroughly alive mentally and physically, I think I would have despaired. No one who has not lived an isolated life can appreciate what it is for a woman. The men had more interest in their lives, for when not scouting they had their "companies" to look after, and when the morning duties were over they could swing a gun over their shoulders and go hunting, which is the greatest pleasure a man knows. We had been at Halleck about one year when the Colonel was ordered to San Francisco as a member of a court-martial; we left the children with Bridget, Dr. Pattey promising to call on the little family every morning and telegraph me their condition. Halleck was about five hundred miles from San Francisco. I had never seen the Sierras and was greatly impressed with their grandeur and beauty. When we were within a few hours of the city we had an accident and were obliged to wait at a small station where there was a bear chained; we fed him and roamed about the place watching for the train that had been telegraphed for. During this time I had observed a little girl about three years old, who ate everything within reach and many more peanuts than the bear. Finally I ventured to speak to the mother about it, who told me, in a manner that plainly said that it was not my affair, that they would not hurt her. At about eight o'clock in the evening the train came. We were soon aboard and ready to move. There were no sleepers. We were all very tired, and most of us asleep, when I heard a frightful scream. On jumping up I found the little girl who had eaten the peanuts in a frightful fit and the mother helpless. I seized the child and ran to the back platform for air, loosened her clothes and bathed her face. A gentleman passenger brought some homeopathic pills, which we got into the child's mouth. It was a terrible sight to me, who loved children so dearly; but by and by she fell quietly asleep; and we all settled down again to get a nap before reaching the city. But there was no sleep for me; the excitement and thinking of my own little ones at the home in the mountains kept me wide awake.

We reached the city at about 10 P.M. and drove to
the Lick House, very tired; but a good night's rest
found us well and ready to go out in the morning.
The city, with its high hills, "Telegraph," "Rincon,"
and "Russian," seemed to form a background for
the bay; there is also a gradual rise in all the streets
back from the bay. To me it was most picturesque,
for from the top of many of the hilly streets could
be seen this most beautiful sheet of water; the harbor of Rio Janeiro being the only one in the world
that can eclipse it.

We wandered about all the morning seeing many
points of interest; after luncheon many of the officers
and their wives came to visit us, also an old friend of
the Colonel's, Major Kettletas, whom he had not seen
since the war, when they had served together in the
Fifteenth Infantry. This officer belonged to one of
the old wealthy families of New York, and at the
breaking out of the war, went in the army, served
with distinction and added new laurels to his family
name; he was brevetted for his gallant services at the
battle of Chickamauga, Georgia, and Mission Ridge,
Tennessee. When peace was declared he resigned and
was travelling on the Pacific Coast when we met him.
He was greatly pleased to see Jim again and gave us
all a dinner at "The Poodle Dog," a famous restaurant, which had been established in the "early

days" by a Frenchman, and called "Le Poulet d'or," but which had been perverted into "The Poodle Dog." Another delightful invitation was to dine with General French and wife and go to a dance afterward given to us by the officers of the Presidio. The ballroom was dressed with flags and lighted by innumerable wax candles stuck on bayonets, which were stacked about the room. It was a beautiful sight, and the music being fine I enjoyed every moment.

I shall never forget the first time I saw the Presidio. I thought I had gotten into Fairyland. The heliotrope grew in such profusion, into great trees, and the fuchsias, that we thought so fine at home when we had a plant three feet high, grew up to the second-story windows and beyond. Roses were in abundance everywhere, and full of bloom. The quarters were all excellent, and there was a most beautiful view of the bay, the islands Alcatraz, Angel, and Yerba Buena, and the Golden Gate. What a garden spot it was for everyone, and especially for children! My enthusiasm knew no bounds, and I greatly regretted that my cavalryman was not in the artillery.

One of the delightful days was spent in going on the steamer " McPherson" to Angel Island, on a picnic given by Mrs. Schofield. It was a most beautiful spot and well deserved its name. The sail from the city and back again, with a number of charming people, was one of the days of my life to be remembered—in fact, each day of the ten spent in this beautiful city stands out in my life in delightful memory.

We returned to Halleck and found the children well and happy. The little Ellen had learned to talk in our absence. I always believed she knew how before, but, as every wish was anticipated (she was watched so closely), she felt it unnecessary; but when we left she began to talk to her nurse.

The life at Halleck after our return was much the same as before, except that Colonel Baker was ordered away and later we moved into the house they had occupied. Here we were much more comfortable, having three large rooms down stairs and two bedrooms above; we had not much furniture, the family being of good size, (and the allowance of luggage small); the Colonel allowed me and the other ladies, each, to have a new iron bedstead from the hospital, in case of a guest coming; otherwise they would have had to sleep there. These bedsteads were kept stored in case they should be needed. After we were settled in our new quarters the Colonel heard that the Inspector General of the Department was coming, so I had the guest room fixed up a little bit. Whatever could be spared from the other rooms was taken in there, fresh muslin curtains were put at the windows, and the canopy I had fixed over the bed covered up the ugly black iron. We had no springs for the bed, but had sacks filled with fresh, sweet hay put under the mattress; it made a comfortable bed, and the room looked very pretty. The Inspector General arrived, and we were glad to see him. He was a charming man socially, was a fine soldier, with a splendid war record, which was considered everything in those days; there was not a better officer in his corps; he was very strict, and almost every post commander dreaded his arrival. The troops and quartermaster's department were inspected, fortunately, the first day; the second day they went to the hospital, which was found in excellent condition, but three new iron bedsteads were missing. The Colonel fully explained their absence; the General listened attentively and then said, " They must be returned immediately; that the Government did not supply beds from the hospital for the use of officers," etc. The bedsteads were at once sent for. Bridget came to me in great distress to know where the Inspector General would sleep? "Make his bed on the floor with the sacks of hay," I replied; "there is no other place." Of course the Colonel thought (if he had time to think of it that day), that I would find some way out of the difficulty, as I usually did when troubles arose. The next morning after the Inspector General's departure the Colonel, in passing the room, saw the bed on the floor and asked what it meant. He was greatly mortified when he learned the Inspector General had slept on the floor, but I thought it just as well for him to realize some of the privations the officers and their families endured who lived on the frontier. Unfortunately the matter got out, as such things do, and was heartily enjoyed at other frontier posts, but it never made any change in our friendship with General Jones, showing he was really a big man. Many years later an officer was presented to me; I bowed, but he put out his hand and said, "I must shake hands with the woman who had the courage to put the dignified Colonel Jones on the floor to sleep."

Not long after this, when we had been at Camp Halleck about eighteen months, I became very ill; our post surgeon did everything he could for me; but, as usual in those days, there were no surgical instruments at the place, and no nurses to be had. When Dr. Brierly found himself helpless he telegraphed to General Schofield telling him the conditions and asking that another surgeon be sent as soon as possible. I continued to grow weaker and weaker. The third day after the telegram had been sent the Colonel received a dispatch, saying the new doctor would arrive that evening and to send a horse to the station for him. But it seemed to be too late; there was no hope left; I had taken the last communion, bade my loved ones good-bye and awaited the end. While hovering between life and death I had a wonderful vision; slowly a beautiful form descended; the face was divine, like the face of the beloved disciple Saint John. The arms were extended, the flowing robe was of the beautiful blue seen in old pictures; it came lower and lower and seemed to say to me, ''All is well!'' I had no power to utter a sound nor to raise my hand.

While waiting for the end, the doctor from San Francisco arrived. He had ridden at a hard gallop the thirteen miles when he learned how desperately ill I was, and to this day he carries the scar of a wound made by a buckle in the saddle, which he would not stop one moment to properly adjust. Such was his idea of duty; he had never seen, probably never heard of, either the Colonel or myself. The sound of his voice as he entered the room seemed to arouse me, and some little time after giving me a stimulant there was a slight pulse, and later I was brought back to life—but had lost my child. It was some time before I was able to recognise anyone, but I well remember the morning when my soul seemed to have come back to me and I opened my eyes and found standing beside my bed a stalwart man, with tawny hair and beard, the picture of health and strength. No wonder I came back from the valley and shadow of Death. He had given me of his strength and compelled me to live. The masterful expression was in his face and I knew I would get well, and quietly whispered it to my husband, who sat beside me.

It was three months before I was able to sit up in bed. The doctor rarely left my bedside, as I required constant watching; but one lovely day I seemed so much better it was thought he could go and have a few hours' shooting. He was a fine hunter and a good shot—in fact, I have since heard that there never was a better sportsman than Dr. George Chismore, and for some little time after this he had a few hours' good shooting every day; but one day he had been gone but a few hours, when a change for the worse came; the orderly rode as fast as possible in the direction the doctor had taken, and in a little while both returned; I was again seriously ill. It was then decided that if my life was to be saved I would have to be taken to the level of the sea; that I could not get well at that altitude. The household things were packed and my husband went first, taking the boys, and got our rooms at the Occidental Hotel. As soon as General Schofield learned the conditions he applied to the War Department to have the Colonel detailed for duty on his staff, so that he might remain near me until the end, for no one thought I would live. The doctor, Bridget, the little Ellen and I followed. I was carried out of the house on a mattress; it seemed as though I was being carried to my grave; and the doctor, seeing a sad expression come over my face, interpreted it at once and said: "We have not got your feet first." Six soldiers carried my mattress and put me in a light spring wagon, covered me up well, and we started, the soldiers going with us. We rode slowly over the sage-brush plains, the odour of which always brings back the memory of the funereal ride; and I never pass Halleck station without going on the platform of the car to see the spot where I spent the fearful night, and which is now, in the imagination of my loved ones, builded into a shrine. It was bitterly cold, and the doctor was afraid I would die before he could get me to the sea. It was my one chance to live, and yet I might not be able to pass the summit of the mountain on our way to the much-desired haven; but I was willing to risk the journey for the one chance offered. In the morning the soldiers carried me again on the mattress into the drawing-room of a Pullman car that had been engaged.

The day passed without change. The summit was passed in the night while I slept, the doctor and nurse watching. There was quite a little rejoicing in the car; the people seemed glad that I had safely passed the Rubicon; and I had many sweet smiles from the passengers as they passed my door. I have often thought since how proud the doctor must have been that he had taken the responsibility and decided it was best to take the one chance that journey gave me.

Years after I was walking on Kearney Street, San Francisco, when a man approached and addressed me, saying: "I never expected to see you alive again; I am one of the men who carried you to the Halleck station when you were so ill. It was a sad day for us all; the boys all turned out of their quarters to see you go by and felt pretty badly." I had always taken great interest in the troop. I often went down and showed the cook how to prepare something nice for the men; they had a fine garden and raised all kinds of vegetables—in fact, one year they made $1200 from their potatoes, which gave them a large company fund. They had a nice mess kit and took pleasure in having everything nice; they also raised pigs, and I remember showing the cook how to make scrapple—a Pennsylvania dish—much to the men's delight, and often I would divide with them the boxes of fruit that were sent me from the city.

One day after we had been in San Francisco a short time, our doctor thought he would take the boys out for a walk and show them the shops and parks and other places of interest. It was all new to them;

they knew nothing but a frontier garrison; the little while we were at home with my parents they had been in the country; so the city was a revelation to them. The men at the street corners with the candy-and-nut stands were all there for them (in their minds) and they insisted upon helping themselves; the doctor had his hands full that afternoon, and I do not remember his inviting them again.

I began to get better from the time we reached the city, but it was two months before I was taken out for a drive; when I was convalescent the Modoc War broke out; and as the troop was going the Colonel applied to go also. He had been temporarily on General Schofield's staff during my illness. It was fully expected the trouble would be settled by the Peace Commissioners and the Colonel, thinking the troops would go no further than Fort Bidwell, California, and as I was far from strong, he decided to take Dave with him. He got the child, who was now nearly six years old, a suit of heavy corduroy and had it re-enforced with buckskin for riding; also some warm underclothing and heavy shoes, in case they should be needed. They went by rail to Elko, Nevada, and there met the troops, and the Colonel got Dave a good pony. The boys, fortunately, had been taught to ride from the time they were four years old, though they were never allowed saddles or stirrups.

Fort Bidwell was beautifully situated, surrounded by mountains. At the top of the highest there was a large lake, covering fully fifty acres, and from this point could be seen thirty-two other lakes. Chief Ocheo lived there with about one hundred braves, and Captain Jack, the Modoc chief at the time of the war, tried his best to persuade Ocheo to join him against the whites; but Ocheo was loyal and would not join him. This chief still lives; he is old and blind. Where the fort stood—which is no longer needed—stands an Indian school, and the boys of this school have built poor old Ocheo a small house. The Government grants him a trifling pension, but it is not sufficient to keep this loyal old chief from want.

Soon after the Colonel and troops reached Bidwell, they received orders to push on, as the Peace Commissioners were not able to adjust the difficulty. It took twelve days, through heavy snow, to reach the lava beds. Three men were frozen so badly they died. Dave rode his pony day after day, just as the soldiers did, and stood the journey well. After reaching the lava beds he and General Canby became great friends. Every day the child went to the hospital to visit the sick and wounded, and went to the funeral of every soldier who succumbed. The soldiers adored him.

One day he and a little Indian boy (about seven

101

years old, who belonged to the troop, having been captured from the Apaches when an infant) went fishing in Tule Lake, quite near the camp. Some Indians fired at them from the lava beds. The Indian boy ran, but, notwithstanding the men called Dave he coolly strung his fish before leaving; the men wanted to run get him, but the Colonel would not allow them to expose themselves, knowing it would bring down a heavier fire. The Colonel had seen General Canby killed. While the Peace Commissioners were in session the General was sent for. He went out of the tent, when two Indians approached and attacked him. Perhaps I can not do better than give General Gillem's report, who was commanding the expedition. He says:

"LAVA BEDS, CAL., April 20, 1873.

"On the morning of the 11th General Canby, with Messrs. Meacham, Thomas, and Dyer, members of the Peace Commission, met the Modoc Indians at a tent pitched about one mile in advance of my camp, at the south end of Tule Lake. The tent was in what is known as the "lava beds." As suspicions of treachery existed, I directed Lieutenant Adams, First Cavalry, chief signal officer, to keep a constant watch on the tent and give me notice of any suspicious movements in its vicinity. The General and members of the commission went out at about 11:06 A.M. At one o'clock I received a message from Major Mason, Twenty-first Infantry, commanding the camp on the east side of the lake, informing me that his pickets had been attacked, and that Lieutenant

Walter Sherwood, Twenty-first Infantry, had been wounded mortally. This confirmed the worst fears of treachery. To notify General Canby of his danger was the first object to be attained, as any movement of troops from the camp would have been in full view of the Indians at the tent. I knew to make an advance would but hasten the attack of the Indians. Acting Assistant Surgeon Cabeniss volunteered to take a message to the General. As many of the Modocs speak English, I had to write. I had written but a line when the signal officer notified me that the Indians were shooting the General and his party. The time elapsing between the attack on Mason's pickets and the attack on General Canby and the Peace Commissioners did not exceed ten minutes, showing conclusively that the action of the Indians was premeditated and preconcerted. The troops in the camp south of the lake at once sprang to their arms and advanced as rapidly as possible to the scene of the tragedy, but the Indians had fled. General Canby and Rev. Mr. Thomas were dead when we reached them; Mr. Meacham was supposed to be mortally wounded, but, I am gratified to state, is rapidly improving, with every probability of an early recovery.

"The party which attacked Major Mason's pickets advanced under a *white flag* and asked for the commanding officer; when asked if they wanted to "talk," they replied "No." Lieutenant Sherwood, the officer of the day, then told them they could return to their camp, and he would return to his; turning to go, the parties being about thirty yards from each other, the Indians opened fire, shooting Lieutenant Sherwood through the arm, and soon afterwards through the thigh, inflicting what proved to be a fatal wound. Lieutenant Boyle, who was with the officer of the day, escaped unhurt; the picket at once opened fire and the Indians fled. . . . ."

This war was one of the hardest Indian campaigns our army has known. There were more officers and soldiers killed for the number of Indians and our men engaged than any other fight. The Indians being intrenched in the lava beds, it was impossible to reach them, while they would take off their clothing, lie flat on the rocks, pick out and fire at every soldier who left his tent; the Indians being the same color of the rocks, it was impossible to see them. My little son completely wore out the clothes he took with him, and the Indian scouts made him a complete suit of buckskin, in which he returned.

While the Colonel was in the lava beds he received his promotion to Major of the Sixth Cavalry, but General Canby had requested him to remain. After being there four months and peace being restored, he returned to San Francisco, *en route* to join his new regiment, and to get me and the children. I was rapidly getting well and strong, notwithstanding the great anxiety of mind. My doctor had been ordered on duty north soon after the Colonel left (and right here I will say that he soon afterward resigned from the army, and, establishing himself in San Francisco, rose to the head of his profession).

I left this unique city with many regrets. For two months after my husband's departure, I was almost a helpless invalid; but my room was kept

104

bright with flowers and the cheerful visits of friends, both army and civilians, who tried to divert my mind from the terrible Indian war. The remains of the young officers killed were brought home and the sad processions out to "Lone Mountain" were to me heart-rending; and I have always thought it hard that the expense of bringing the bodies of these gallant fellows home had to be borne by their young wives, who could not think of leaving them to be buried where they fell, perhaps to be mutilated later by these wretched Indians. Of course, General Canby's body was taken home by the Government, and his remains were honored by this city (San Francisco) on the way East. Shops were closed, no business done, and the citizens turned out *en masse* to form an escort; it was a sad day for every one.

I cannot leave this dear city by the Golden Gate without speaking of the General commanding the Department. He was most considerate in sending me the war news every day, and I have never forgotten his great kindness during the seven months of my illness. He was equally thoughtful of the wives and families of the officers who were in the lava beds fighting, and I doubt if any commanding officer was ever more beloved than General Schofield at that time.

CHAPTER VI.

We arrived at Fort Riley, Kansas, after an uneventful ride across the alkali plains. I was heartily
glad to go immediately into our own quarters; our
furniture having been sent on from Fort Halleck
before we left San Francisco. We got women to
clean the quarters selected, and were rapidly getting
settled, when the Colonel got a telegram ordering
him to Leavenworth, the headquarters of the Department. On his arriving there, General Pope told him
that he was to go to Fort Lyon, Colorado, in command
of the post. Our things were all to be repacked and
many of our steps retraced; the fatigue of the family
and extra expense were things not counted. I needed
a cook and housemaid, and knowing there were none
to be had on the plains went to Junction City, close
by, to look for them, going in all the shops and offering, at that date, very high wages, but could hear
of no one; finally I decided to go and see the Catholic
priest, as I knew he would be acquainted with all the
young women in his parish. He received me kindly
and took an interest in the matter, and when we left
I took with me a young Irish girl named Mary

Broderick, whose brother was a farmer, and she had lived with him and his wife. The priest afterward sent me another excellent young woman named Sarah McDermott, Mary's cousin.

The journey to Fort Lyon was full of interest. We went by the Atchison and Topeka Railway, which was then new. There had been heavy rains and floods, and we travelled slowly, seeing countless antelopes and buffaloes. The train actually stopped while some English and American tourists shot a few of them; it was most exciting. Dodge City was then the terminus of the road, a terrible little frontier town. On arriving we went to the hotel to remain over night. It was a wooden building, without paint or wash of any kind, with two front doors, one leading into a saloon, the other into a parlor. There was a yellowish green ingrain carpet on the floor, a "suit" of furniture covered with majenta plush with yellow figures in it, coarse Nottingham lace curtains at the windows and some vivid chromos on the walls. The children, maids and I entered this room, while the Colonel went in search of the host. He soon returned and with him a woman with a hard face, fully six feet tall and of very large frame. She was dressed in a "bloomer" costume—full blue trousers drawn in at the ankle, and a long blue sacque reaching nearly to the knee; a knife and pistol were in her belt.

107

While she talked to me Dave got up in the middle of the room and, pointing at her, laughed aloud and said: "Look at her, Jack; isn't she funny? Look at the knife, Jack." I was terrified lest she would kill him, but she quietly turned to him and said: "Come with me and get some cake and milk." I was afraid to let him go, but his father had nodded consent, and away he went. Poor Jack, who had not laughed at her audibly, was not invited.

After supper, which was not bad (but the first time I had eaten buffalo meat), we went to our rooms, in the second story of the house, reached by narrow open steps. There was one big room divided two-thirds of the way up into smaller rooms by white heavy muslin stretched across, all open at the top. There was a wooden bedstead, chair and small table with pitcher and basin on it in each room; the latter was about 6 x 10 feet. The children, maids and I went to bed, for we were tired; the Colonel came later, as there were many soldiers around and he wanted to keep his eye on the man who was to drive us the next day to Fort Lyon.

Fort Dodge was about five miles distant, and the soldiers on pass came to the town, drank villanous whiskey which these saloons kept, and after a drink or two the men would be crazy drunk, their clothes and everything they had with them stolen, and when

the saloon-keepers had gotten all they possessed they
were thrown out into the streets. This was before
the days of the canteen, which remedied everything
for the time; but the liquor dealers were too strong
for the law-makers, and the canteen, where no whiskey was sold, had to go, so the conditions are about
the same as before; there is always a grog-shop on
the outskirts of every garrison.

About midnight we were all awakened by pistol
shots. The Colonel was in his clothes and downstairs
in a minute. There was a genuine fight on hand,
pistols and knives being used. The floor of our rooms
and the ceiling of the saloon was but one board thick,
so we heard it all and feared some of the shots might
reach us. The Colonel returned after a time, when
all was quiet, but there was not much sleep to be had,
and I was heartily glad to have an early breakfast
and shake the dust of Dodge City from my feet. I
am told it is now a flourishing city.

We had a comfortable ambulance, four mules, and
a good driver. The Colonel sat in front with the
driver, to be on the lookout; we had no escort, excepting the few men on the baggage-waggons; the Indians
just at this time were considered peaceful. The ride
was most interesting. We saw great herds of
buffaloes, antelopes, and much small game, which the
Colonel occasionally shot for our meals. Once when

we were about to ford the stream we waited for some
buffaloes to cross, but when our driver found it was an
unusually large herd and our mules very restive we
drove a mile or two along the bank and made a
crossing. We could see across these plains for many,
many miles, owing to the condition of the atmosphere.
The country was entirely different from the sage-
brush plains of Nevada, and the mountains were far
in the distance, but nothing can be more monotonous
and drear than the aspect of these prairies; nothing
meets the eye but the expanse of arid waste, not a
tree or shrub to be seen except on the little streams
where the cottonwood grows. Shortly before arriving
at the post, a young cavalry officer rode up and, dis-
mounting, introduced himself to the Colonel (who
had gotten down from the ambulance) as Lieutenant
George S. Anderson, Sixth Cavalry. Although he had
never before met us, he had ridden out about fifteen
miles to welcome us to Fort Lyon, and to offer us the
use of his quarters until we could get ours in order.
It pleases me to think that the friendship begun that
day, on the desolate Western prairie, has never been
broken.

Fort Lyon was an ideal post. There were four
companies of Third Infantry and two troops of the
Sixth Cavalry; Captain Rafferty (long since dead)
and Lieutenants Perrine and Anderson; Lieutenant

QUARTERS AT FORT LYON, COLORADO

Wallace was in command of his troop, the captain being away on other duty; Colonel J. Ford Kent, Captain Stouch, Lieutenant Hanna, and many others. There were also many ladies—Mrs. Page, a charming woman, wife of Captain John H. Page; Mrs. Happersett, the life almost of the garrison, wife of the surgeon; Mrs. Wallace and dear little George, Mrs. Stouch, Mrs. Hanna and Daisy, the family of chaplain, Mrs. Latourette, and others.

The commanding officer's quarters were better than any we had ever had. It was an adobe house with a wide porch; there were two rooms, sixteen feet square, on each side of a wide hall; kitchen and pantry in the back; also four very good rooms on the second floor. We had sent East for carpets, curtains and other necessary things. There were fine wardrobes and drawers built in the bedrooms and a sideboard in the dining-room, besides some tables, bedsteads—rather rough, to be sure; but with some coats of paint and canopies of white muslin over the bedsteads and dressing-tables, clean white curtains at the windows, the rooms were soon made to look dainty and pretty.

An amusing incident occurred soon after our arrival. On unpacking the clock, I found it would not go. Lieutenant Anderson, being present, suggested sending it to the doctor, who loved to set clocks to rights. That afternoon I told Jack to take the clock to Dr. Davis and ask him if he would kindly see what was the matter with it? The Doctor had joined the regiment a few days before ourselves and it was his first experience as an army surgeon. Many of his friends had teased him about going in the service and told him he would be called upon to attend the pet cats and dogs, but none had mentioned that he would have to doctor the clocks; however, he took a look at it and found a small stick had been put across to keep the pendulum from moving. Taking this out, the clock went all right, later he sent it in to me; the Colonel was present when the man brought it in and asked where it had been? He was horrified when he learned to whom I had sent it. Lieutenant Anderson had meant me to send it to Lieutenant Perrine, who was always called "Doctor" at West Point, and the name had clung to him; of course, the Colonel apologised to the young doctor.

One day several of us were sitting by the big open wood fire, and the dogs, "Beauty," a fine Irish setter, and "Don," a pointer, lay on the hearth enjoying the fire also, when they heard their master's voice outside; in an instant "Beauty" made a bound, and seeing the door shut she went through the lace curtain and pane of glass, and "Don" followed after her, going through the same hole. Neither of them was hurt; the curtain dragged after them and protected them from the broken glass. They evidently thought the Colonel was going hunting without them, as they had watched him clean his gun in the early morning. Dogs that live closely with a family as ours did become very human, and know all that is talked about, especially anything that concerns them.

The first summer we were at Fort Lyon was a very gay one. My niece, Kate Caldwell, came to spend the summer with us. General and Mrs. Perrine, Mrs. Bell and dear little Annie came to visit Lieutenant Perrine. Mrs. Page had her sister-in-law, Mrs. Tracy, and pretty little Sophie Sloane, just budding into womanhood. Mr. Hodding and Mr. Clutton, Englishmen, who had a ranch on the Cimarron, near Pueblo, were visiting Dr. Happersett, and Mr. William Fanshawe, of New York, who also had a ranch on the Cimarron, was visiting us. The girls enjoyed every moment thoroughly. There were horseback rides, and drives, dances, card parties, charades, and every kind of entertainment that we all could devise. The weather was perfect and there was nothing to disturb our pleasure; in fact, dear old General Perrine said it was nearer Arcadia than he had ever expected to see.

One day Jack came and told me that a Roman Catholic priest was on the porch and would like to see me. I immediately went to the door, and there was Father Darasch from Junction City; he had come all the way to look after the two girls of his parish, to see what kind of a home they had and how they were doing; he had felt the responsibility of sending them away. This impressed me deeply. We invited the good Father to stop several days with us, which he did. The Colonel arranged with him to have service for the men, and in fact we all attended—officers and ladies, having such great respect for the man. He was indeed the father of his flock.

I remember with great pleasure a dance, or "baile," as the Mexicans call a dance. It was given at a ranch about eight miles from the post. When Kit Carson, the noted Indian scout of many years ago, died, he left several children entirely unprovided for. Mr. Boggs, who owned a large ranch in Colorado, adopted two or three of these children as his own, and it was the wedding reception of the eldest to which we were invited. The Colonel at first thought I had better not go; he thought there might be Mexicans there with whom I might not care to dance, should they ask me; and he would not have me hurt their feelings by declining; but I had no such thought; I was very anxious to go and meet the people, so I went with the officers and their wives and took my niece. I shall never forget it, nor my dance with the Dutch baker. The dance I believe was the schottische. He was short and very fat.

After a slide, in which we bent low (for I did just as he did), we hopped three times on one foot; another slide back and hopped again; then such a swing around as he gave me—it nearly took me off my feet; he was delighted that I had learned his dance, much to the amusement of many present. Such a supper as we had one rarely sees: quantities of all kinds of game, turkeys and chickens, beef and mutton, all kinds of wine and spirits—a feast of the olden time. It was here that the babies were mixed up. When we arrived we were all ushered into a large room to take off our wraps. There was a very large bedstead in the room, and on each side of the bed, lying close together well wrapped up, were babies belonging to the different Mexican women who were at the ball. It occurred to some of the mischief-loving young people late in the evening to change the places of the babies, those at the top being put at the bottom and those at the bottom put in the middle and so on. What was the after effect I never heard.

The following autumn a great excitement prevailed. Several hundreds of the Southern Cheyennes came within a few miles of the post. They said they had come to fight the Utes, but it was generally supposed to be a cattle-stealing expedition. The ladies and children were not allowed to go outside the garrison, and the young children were lariated (tied) with long ropes to the flagstaff, so they could not get out of sight. One day some officers were going to the Indian camp. Mrs. Happersett, my niece and I begged to go along; we thought we would not be afraid going with officers and men, but when we got there and saw those terrible looking creatures, with such brutal faces, I felt far from comfortable. The older women were most repulsive in appearance; their faces were full of deep lines, showing the hardships they must have endured; their ears had been pierced, and those that were not torn in great slits had heavy pieces of silver in different shapes hanging in them, they put their hands on us and felt my cheeks and hair and insisted upon my taking it down for them to see, but I was afraid as several of the Indians were climbing up on our ambulance wheels begging Kate, my niece, for the feathers in her hat, which she gave them, also a string of amber beads, with which they were delighted; in return they gave her a pair of broad silver bracelets, very well engraved with Indian characters. After the Indians had been camped for several days, the Colonel received orders from General Pope to send them back to their reservation. The order was obeyed reluctantly, but, of course, they had to go.

As I have said, we were not allowed to walk or ride outside the garrison while the Indians were camped so near; but several days after they had been ordered to their reservation Dr. Happersett, the surgeon, came and asked me to drive with his wife, Mrs. Page and himself. The Doctor had a fine pair of spirited black horses, and I was always glad to ride behind them, and especially that day as we had not been riding or driving for so long a time. We went out on the old Santa Fé road. The afternoon was delightful, and we were all in fine spirits. The sunset was gorgeous—great streaks of gold and red, heliotrope, orange and blue. The Doctor spoke of returning, but I could not bear to turn my back on that wonderful sky and begged that we should go slowly on. All at once we came to a stop; the left front wheel would not revolve. I took the reins while the Doctor jumped down to find the cause, and he soon discovered a hot-box; his man had taken the wheels off that day to grease them and had gotten one on wrong. After losing much time trying to get the wheel off, without effect, the Doctor decided it best to mount one of the horses, if possible (for they had never been ridden), get to the fort as quickly as he could and send an ambulance out for us. We were about four miles out, and as none of us were robust, the Doctor thought it impossible for us to walk the distance, though we suggested doing so, but the Doctor considered it best for us to sit in the carriage, which we did for a time.

117

The twilight is very short in Colorado, and it soon began to grow dark; so it seemed to me best that we start toward the garrison and meet the ambulance. We walked on, each giving experiences on similar occasions to ourselves or others we had known, and each feeling, without telling the other, a good bit scared, wondering if there were any straggling Indians about; it was now dark, and it was the blackest night before the August moon rose that I had ever seen; we could not see the road and stopped every little while to feel whether we were on the road or on the grassy plains. Suddenly we heard a noise which seemed to come out of the earth, and some one spoke to us. We could not understand what was said and I halted a moment, when the voice spoke again. In an instant Mrs. Happersett gave a terrifying scream and ran, Mrs. Page and I following, she clinging to me almost fainting from fright. We could hear the steps of men close behind us. There seemed to be two or three or more. We kept on the grass off the road and made no sound; the blackness of the night saved us. They could not see which way we were going. After running a long distance we came to a cross roads, which we knew by feeling the earth, and hearing no sounds of men behind us we sat down on the ground, not knowing which road to take. It was not very long before we heard the

sound of horses' hoofs but we did not speak, only
pressed each other's hand. The sound came closer
and closer, and by and by we saw a man on a horse
coming toward us. He held a lantern in one hand
which he raised from time to time looking about,
and as he got nearer we saw it was young Latourette.
The Doctor had met him as he rode into the garrison
and told him where we were and for him to ride out
as rapidly as possible and stay with us. The lad
could not understand meeting us so close to the fort.
While we were talking we heard a moan. After lis-
tening attentively we thought it must be Mrs. Happersett and with the aid of the lantern Mr. Latourette
found her where she had dropped in the road from
exhaustion. Both she and Mrs. Page fell on young
Latourette's neck and wept, while I tried to tell what
had happened. We sat by the roadside waiting, and
after what appeared to us a long time we heard the
rumbling of wheels. We waved our lantern and the
ambulance stopped. Lieutenant Anderson had come
for us; fortunately he was big and strong, for he had
to lift each one of us into the waggon, and when we
reached the garrison we were utterly exhausted
with fright and fatigue. After hearing our experience the Colonel sent a sergeant and some men out
on the road to hunt for the men who had frightened
us, but they found no one. The Colonel thought they

were not Indians, but possibly two of a band of horse thieves that had broken out of the guard-house early that morning, by getting through the roof, although they were manacled. It was some days before we recovered from the fright, and I never pass over the old Santa Fé road, or see a brilliant western sunset, without recalling the terrors of that black August night.

Las Animas was a small town about five miles above the fort, and we went there to do our shopping, or for a drive. We had but the two roads, this one and the old Sante Fé trail, which is still good and full of interest. Las Animas had been settled by very respectable people, and I have the pleasure of knowing that I started the fund for the first little Episcopal church built there. I remember going one morning in the Colonel's ambulance with four fine mules, and had all of my children with me; it was in the Spring and the children stopped to gather the wild flowers, the verbena in all colours and the little forget-me-nots. We had had a cold winter, the ground covered with snow most of the time, and it was a delight to the children to see these little flowers putting their heads above ground. When we got to the ford the water was very high. The bridge over the river (Arkansas) had been washed away the year before. As we went over my driver said he thought the river was rapidly rising, but I, not thinking much about it, went on and leisurely attended to my shopping, and then started for the fort. On reaching the ford where we usually crossed the river was rushing madly, and the man hesitated about crossing, but I, not realising the danger, told him to go on, and we started. In a moment I saw our peril. The mules struggled and swam, the body of the ambulance was filled with water up to the seats. We were carried by the current far below the ford, but after a desperate struggle of both driver and mules we reached the other bank, thoroughly frightened and thoroughly wet. It taught me a lesson, never to ford a rapidly rising stream.

The Arkansas River flows southeast through Colorado a distance of five hundred miles and is navigable at no point, but in the spring it rises suddenly, and often does great damage. There is also a pretty little stream flowing near Las Animas, called the "Purgatoire," but which the settlers call "The Picketwire."

Late that autumn we had a delightful visit from General Sheridan, General Forsyth and Colonel Sheridan. The General was on an inspecting tour. It was a great pleasure to me to see these officers again and to have the opportunity of entertaining them in my own house. I had not seen them since those dear, delightful days in New Orleans. There was so much to talk over. The General was in great good spirits; it was shortly before his marriage to the beautiful Miss Rucker. We thoroughly enjoyed this little visit. They brightened us up wonderfully, coming as they did from the outside world. The Colonel had plenty of game for them. He was always a fine shot and kept the ladies supplied with all they wanted. We had a rope stretched across the cellar; the birds were tied two together and thrown across the rope; anyone could go in and help themselves; the only rule was, they must take them as they came and not pick out the best of the lot.

Shortly after General Sheridan's visit Colonel DeLancy Floyd Jones came to see us. He came to inspect the four companies of his regiment at our post. He was a charming man and guest, and when he returned to Fort Wallace he sent his band to spend a week at our garrison to give us all the music we wanted. Of course, this was an occasion for dinners and dances. I well remember a mask ball we gave. Some of the ladies' costumes were very handsome and some of the officers' were certainly unique. Lieutenant Anderson, who was six feet two or three inches tall, went as a skeleton. His costume was of heavy black goods and was painted in white, the mask being painted as a skull. Captain Hentig went as the

"Evil Eye." He was also in black, with one eye, and really scared me whenever he approached. Poor fellow, he was afterwards killed by Indians. Then there was a harlequin, and the devil, the latter Lieutenant Perrine, who was sewed up in red and painted with white and phosphorus. These were the most startling, and no one knew them. There were no strangers present, only our own garrison and some officers and ladies, whom we all knew, from other posts not far off. We all contributed to the supper, which was fine; the Colonel made the punch, which guaranteed it. Of course, we invited Colonel Floyd Jones, as we could not have had the ball without his generosity in sending the band.

One Sunday afternoon, at about three o'clock, I was writing, and it suddenly grew dark. I thought a storm was approaching; we frequently had fierce wind-storms and would see the dark gray angry-looking clouds some time before the storm would reach us, when the sergeant of the guard would send some men to close the heavy wooden shutters, and we would light the lamps until it was over; but this afternoon it looked very queer, and in a little while it became perfectly dark. The sky was obscured by grasshoppers. They came in great clouds and ate everything in their passage. We all had vines over our porches, and not a leaf was left. They ate the troop gardens, hundreds of watermelons not yet ripe; in fact, not a blade of grass remained. They were all night and the whole of the next day in passing.

One morning the Colonel started out to take the morning report at "reveille," as was his custom during the long years of service. He found we had had a tremendous storm and the snow was banked high against the front of the house, making it impossible to get out; so he decided to go by the back gate. When he opened the door, he heard "Comet," his favorite horse, who had won many a quarterstretch on the race course, stamping and neighing, and on going to the stable found him greatly excited over something. After quieting him down a little, Colonel started to go out of the gate but could not open it, although it gave a little and felt as though someone were leaning hard against it. Thinking it might be a soldier, he climbed as well as he could to the top, and to his great astonishment saw a buffalo against it. A herd of them had come in for protection from the storm. As many as possible were along the fence and they were all crowded together. The children in the garrison were all greatly excited over them as, indeed, we all were. These were the last buffaloes I saw during my life on the plains.

I well remember escorting a troop on its first day's march when going on a scout. The officers had invited the girls, and they thought it would be "so lovely" to ride out with them about fifteen miles and camp for the night. They talked so much about it, that Mrs. Page and I decided to give them the coveted experience they so desired. They were several days preparing for the trip. Enough food was cooked and taken for a regiment. We got off early one morning and had a very good ride until about eleven o'clock, when we stopped for luncheon; after which we started off again. The wind having come up quite strong, it was not so pleasant riding; and by four o'clock when we stopped to camp for the night a hurricane was blowing great clouds of dust. We could not see our hands before us, and it was almost impossible for the men to put up the tent for us. Nothing could be taken from the hampers that so much time had been spent in preparing for the anticipated banquet. We ate our supper a small piece at a time, with our veils drawn down tight over our faces to keep from getting our "peck of dust" all in a moment. The ladies, six of us, were all huddled in one tent for the night, while Lieutenant Perrine, Lieutenant Anderson and two soldiers spent the night holding down the four corners of the tent; the ropes were well wrapped about the pegs, but it was as nothing against the violence of the storm on the desert. Next morning, after a cup of good coffee, but a light breakfast, we mounted

our horses, bade the officers "Good-bye," and with
the two "orderlies" retraced our steps to the fort,
the wind having greatly subsided. If memory serves
me right, I heard nothing more that summer about
the delights of escorting a troop on its first day's
march.

My dear friend, Dr. Chismore, who lived a long
time with the Indians of Nevada, Colorado, California, and Alaska, and who was selected to accompany
Lady Franklin to Alaska in search of Sir John's
body, on account of the numerous Indian dialects he
spoke, told me of a most interesting tradition of the
Arapaho and Comanche Indians of Colorado, which
he had translated while living among them. All
Indians possess legends to account for any extraor-
dinary occurrences, or natural phenomena which they
do not understand, and their legendary version of
the causes which created in the midst of their hunt-
ing-ground—to the northwest of Fort Lyon—two
springs, one of sweet and the other of bitter water,
was the cause of the tribes of the Comanches and
Snakes separating.

"Many hundreds of winters ago, when the tribes
of Indians were all at peace, two hunters of different
nations chanced to meet one day by a small stream
where both had gone to quench their thirst; a little
stream of water rising from a spring within a few

feet of the bank, flowed over it and fell into the river. To this the hunters walked, and while one went to the spring itself the other, tired by his exertions in the chase, threw himself on the ground and plunged his face into the running stream. The latter had not been successful in the chase, and his bad fortune and the sight of the game which the other hunter threw from his back before he drank at the crystal spring caused a feeling of jealousy to take possession of his mind. The other, before he had satisfied his thirst, raised in the hollow of his hand some of the water and lifting it first toward the sun poured it upon the ground—a libation to the Great Spirit who had given him a successful hunt, and the blessing of the refreshing water which he was about to drink. Seeing this, and being reminded that he had neglected the usual offering, only made him more angry, and the evil spirit at that moment entering his body got the mastery of him and he tried to provoke a quarrel with the strange Indian.

" 'Why does a stranger,' he asked, rising from the stream, 'drink at the spring-head, when one to whom the fountain belongs contents himself with the water that runs from it?'

" 'The Great Spirit places the cool water at the spring,' answered the other hunter, 'that his children may drink it pure and undefiled. The running water is for the beasts which scour the plains; Au-sa-qua is a chief of the Shos-shone: he drinks at the head water.'

" 'The Shos-shone is but a tribe of the Comanche,' returned the other; 'Waco-mish leads the grand nation. Why does a Shos-shone dare to drink above him?'

" 'He has said it. The Shos-shone drinks at the spring head; Au-sa-qua is chief of his nation. The Comanche are brothers, let them both drink of the same water.'

" ' The Shos-shone pays tribute to the Comanche, Waco-mish leads that nation to war, Waco-mish is chief of the Shos-shone, as he is of his own people.'

" 'Waco-mish lies; his tongue is forked like a rattle-snake; his heart is black as the Misho-tunga (bad spirit). When the Manitou made his children, whether Shos-shone or Comanche, Arapaho, Shi-an or Paine, he gave them buffalo to eat, and the pure water of the fountain to drink. He said not to one, drink here, and to another, drink there; but he gave the spring to all, that all might drink.'

"Waco-mish almost burst with rage as the other spoke; but his coward heart prevented him from attacking the calm Shos-shone. He, made thirsty by the words he had spoken—for the red man is usually quiet—stooped down to the spring to quench

128

his thirst, when the subtle warrior of the Comanche threw himself upon the kneeling hunter and forcing his head into the bubbling water held him down with all his strength, until he fell forward over the spring, drowned and dead. The murderer stood looking at the body, and no sooner was the deed done than bitter remorse took possession of him; with hands clasped to his forehead he stood gazing intently on his victim, whose head still remained in the fountain. Mechanically he dragged the body a few steps from the water; as soon as the head of the dead Indian was withdrawn, the Comanche saw the water suddenly and strangely disturbed. Bubbles sprung up from the bottom, and rising to the surface escaped in hissing gas; a thin vapoury cloud rose and, gradually dissolving, displayed to the eyes of the trembling murderer the figure of an aged Indian, whose long snowy hair and venerable beard, blown aside by a gentle wind from his breast, showed the well-known totem of the great Wan-kan-aga, the father of the Comanche and Shos-shone nation whom the tradition of the tribe, handed down by skilful hieroglyphics, almost deified for the good actions and deeds of bravery this famous warrior had performed on earth. Stretching out a war-club toward the frightened murderer, the figure thus addressed him: 'Accursed of my tribe! this day thou hast severed the link between

the mightiest nations in the world, while the blood
of the brave Shos-shone cries to the Manitou for ven-
geance. May the water of thy tribe be rank and
bitter in their throats.' Thus saying and swinging
his ponderous war-club around his head he dashed
out the brains of the Comanche, who fell headlong
into the spring, which from that day to this remains
rank and bitter, so that even when one is half dead
with thirst he cannot drink the water of the foul
spring.

"The good Wan-kan-aga, however, to perpetuate
the memory of the Shos-shone warrior, who was re-
nowned in his tribe for valor, struck with the same
avenging club a hard flat rock, which overhung the
stream, just out of sight of this scene of blood; and
straightway the rock opened into a round clear basin,
which instantly filled with sparkling water, and no
thirsty hunter ever drank a cooler or sweeter draught.
The two streams remain an everlasting monument of
the foul murder of the brave Shos-shone, and the
stern justice of the good Wan-kan-aga; and from
that day the two great tribes of the Shos-shone and
Comanche have remained apart; a long and bloody
war followed the murder of the Shos-shone chief and
many a Comanche paid the penalty of death."

The following August (1874) the Colonel, with his
battalion, joined Colonel (now General) Nelson A.

Yours faithfully
Atnot Shaffer
Lt. Genl usa retd.

Miles, leaving me and the children at Fort Lyon not knowing the extent of the uprising, but the campaign proved to be a very severe one and lasted about sixteen months. The Kiowas, Comanches and Cheyennes had left their reservations and joined together for this campaign; there were also the Cherokees, Arapahos, Chickasaws and many other tribes that were warlike and had to be subdued. The command marched to "Camp Supply," meeting Indians and fighting continually on their way; from there they marched to the Staked Plains, in the extreme northwest of Texas, where Colonel Biddle located "Fort Elliott." The weather was bitterly cold, at times thirty degrees below zero, and their sufferings were great; they were obliged to tie up their feet and ankles with straw; many of the men had their hands and feet frozen. They slept on the ground in their blankets with no tents and nothing to shelter them from the storms. I have often heard my husband in talking of this campaign speak of the gallant charge Captain (now General) Chaffee made in a fight near the Red River. There were several hundred warriors and Chaffee and his men charged up a hill at least two hundred feet high, where he carried the position. The fighting was so close that the men used their pistols. Lieutenant Anderson, who had been Colonel Biddle's adjutant, was also in this fight. He had been sent with a message to Captain Chaffee and remained to take part, riding beside Captain Chaffee up the hill. It was also in this campaign that four white girls named Germaine were rescued from the Cheyenne Indians. They were from Georgia and were *en route* to Colorado when they were attacked near Smoky Hill River. The father, mother and two children were killed, and the four girls taken captives; two were quite young and two grown up. They were taken by the Indians to the Cheyenne village where they were finally rescued by the Sixth Cavalry. I have been told that our Government made provision for them. It may be interesting to hear Colonel Neill's report:

"Lieutenant Colonel Thomas H. Neill, Sixth Cavalry, commanding a camp near the Cheyenne Agency, sent an Indian runner to 'Stone Calf's' village with this note: 'Jan. 20th, 1875. To Katharine Elizabeth, or to Sophia Louisa Germain, white woman, now in the hands of the hostile Cheyennes with 'Grey Beard' or 'Stone Calf.' I send you these few lines to tell you that your younger sisters, Juliana and Nancy, are safe and well and have been sent home to Georgia. Your sad captivity is known all over the country and every effort to obtain your release will be made. Read this note to Stone Calf or Grey Beard, and say to Stone Calf that his message has been received, and that I will receive him and his band upon condition that he shall send you and your sister in first, and then he can come in with his band and give himself up to the mercy of the Government and I will receive him. I send you with this, pencil and paper; write me Stone Calf's answer, and anything else you may desire; I think the Indians will make no objection."

I remained at Fort Lyon for several months with my little family, thinking each month the troops would come home; and, besides, I could get more news of the campaign here. The Third Infantry had gotten orders to go to Louisiana, and we saw them off with great regret. The Nineteenth Infantry, commanded by Colonel Charles Smith, arrived in their place. This regiment, up to that time, had seen no Indian service, having been stationed in the South during the reconstruction. I well remember the first Indian excitement that occurred after the Sixth had gone and the Nineteenth was installed. One morning a runner came dashing into the garrison with the news that a large band of Indians (presumably Cheyennes) were within five miles of Las Animas. The troops were soon dispatched to send these renegades back to their reservations. If they refused to return, of course a fight would ensue. Colonel Smith got all the big guns on the parade ready for action and sent rifles to all of our houses for us to protect ourselves and children in case of necessity, for the majority of the officers had gone out with their companies and there were barely enough soldiers left to protect the garrison in case

of an attack. During the day we were not so much
alarmed, for we could see across the plains for so
many miles, but when the shadows of night fell our
hearts went down too, and there was but little sleep
for men or women in that isolated army post. Late
the next day the troops returned. They had over-
taken a small band of Indians (who had greatly
alarmed the settlers) but they were persuaded after
a short parley (and the sight of soldiers armed ready
for them in case of refusal) to return peaceably to
their reservation, an escort being sent with them.
We soon quieted down and forgot our fright, but the
reports had gotten to the newspapers in the East, and
had lost nothing in transit. My parents, therefore,
were greatly worried and insisted upon my returning
home with my children, so we packed up our furniture, gave it to the quartermaster for storage
and turned our faces eastward. My niece, who
had been staying with me, was fond of collecting
butterflies, horned toads, curious insects of all kinds,
as well as remarkable snakes, and she had a large and,
I have no doubt, a valuable collection, for the soldiers
of the Sixth Cavalry were always on the lookout for
anything unusual for her. Kate was a tall handsome
girl of sixteen. She rode well, drove four in hand,
went shooting with her uncle and other officers, and
was an all round good comrade, and the soldiers, as

well as every one who knew her, were fond of her.
Often before breakfast a soldier would come to the
house and ask if Miss Kate would ride his horse that
morning. When she would accept, the horse would
be brought to the house fairly shining. She had her
own horse, but the men seemed to feel quite honoured
when she rode theirs. But to return to Kate's snakes,
which she kept in alcohol in large-mouthed bottles.
I was very much afraid of them and told her she
could not take them home, as they could not be packed
and we had too much to carry. She seemed to acqui-
esce and I did not think of them again. When we
started on our journey each one was assigned a
special bag, bundle or box to look after and carry
until we reached our destination; mine was the carriage blanket, rolled nicely as the soldiers roll their
blankets. After our arrival home, Kate was talking
with her grandfather about the wonderful reptiles
in Colorado and he seemed to think she was "drawing
a long bow"; when, to my astonishment, she said:
"Well, I will show them to you;" which she did. I
had carried them home wrapped in the carriage-rug,
which had been given to me to look after on our trip.
Of course, Kate and the children enjoyed the joke.

My children at this time were little frontiermen.
The sight of fruit growing or a cultivated garden
they had not seen since old enough to remember, and

their excitement was intense and their remarks curious when they saw these beautiful sights. As we passed through Kansas the lads saw an apple orchard, the trees laden with the ripe red fruit; their enthusiasm was great and they called out: "Look at the wild apples growing on trees." As we neared home the train stopped at a small town in New Jersey where we saw from the car-window an old church-yard, with beautiful weeping willow trees and old and new monuments. Nelly, now nearly four years old, exclaimed in great delight: "Oh! Mama, look at the beautiful stones growing out there!" I tried to explain that they were placed there to mark the graves where people were buried, when again she said in a loud voice: "Grave-stones? What are grave-stones? And why didn't we have them where we lived?" The people in the car rose and looked at us, so I thought they might as well be puzzled a little more, and said: "Dear child, the people did not die where we lived." It was the truth. We had never seen a funeral while we were in Colorado.

When we got off the car a few miles further on, many of the passengers got off to take a last look at us, and I think they were a bit surprised to see a tall, handsome, elderly gentleman meet us with a fine turnout, ready to drive us home. What may also have added to the curiosity of the passengers was the fact that I was wearing a large, old-fashioned bonnet that I had taken West with me years ago. The styles had changed and the women were wearing little three-cornered patches, called "Fanchons." I was unconscious that I was not in the fashion, until I saw my sisters, who met me with raised hands, exclaiming, before greeting me: "Where in the world did your bonnet come from? You look as though you had just escaped from the Ark." I was inclined to feel a little hurt at first, but after seeing their pretty little hats I enjoyed the joke and no longer wondered why the people had looked at me as they did.

After this campaign, which lasted for more than a year, the Colonel applied for a three-months' "leave"—he had not been away from duty since the autumn of 1869—but, instead of getting the "leave" which he had been looking forward to, he received the following letter from General Pope:

HEADQUARTERS OF THE DEPARTMENT OF THE MISSOURI,
LEAVENWORTH, KANSAS,
December 17th, 1874.
MY DEAR MAJOR:

It has been with great reluctance, and only because I could not in any view of the public interest avoid it, that I have felt obliged to assign you to the command of the cantonment on the Sweetwater. For such a command a cavalry officer of experience in that arm of service and good judgment was absolutely needed, and your assignment was forced upon me. The command is the largest and most important in the Department and gives opportunity for valuable and noteworthy service. By the 1st of May your duty will come to an end and you will come in. Whatever I can do to promote any wishes you may have for the spring or summer I will do very gladly, and meantime I feel confident you will administer this important command with vigor and success.

Very truly yours,

(Signed) JNO. POPE.

Major BIDDLE, U. S. A.

The Colonel remained at the cantonment until the following June. He and his command were the first white people to enter that barren and barbarous region, in the extreme northwest of Texas, called the Panhandle; it is now thickly settled and prosperous. After the fort was established and all in that section quiet, the Colonel was relieved from duty and given a four-months' "leave." It was a great joy to his old father, who had not long to live, to see him again, and we made plans for a pleasant summer. But, alas! for the plans. He had been home but a few weeks when he received a letter from General Sheridan, reading as follows:

CHICAGO, July 9th, 1875.

MY DEAR MAJOR BIDDLE:

I was obliged to revoke the promise for your additional two months, for the reason that the Sixth Cavalry was going into a new depot, without, or, at least, with but one field officer, and

138

I felt that I would not be doing justice to my own sense of what I consider my duty to let this be done, and therefore revoked the authority and asked you back, so that the regiment might have two field officers. I was very sorry to inconvenience one for whom I have the highest regard, personally and officially.

With kind regards to Mrs. Biddle and the ladies I met with her at Fort Lyon, I am,   Yours truly,

(Signed) P. H. SHERIDAN.

Although the letter was complimentary, it did not at that time lessen the trial to me or the children. The Colonel had been to the tailor (the first thing an officer does on leave) and gotten an entire outfit of civilian clothes, which were never worn, as it was seventeen years before he had another "leave," being constantly in Arizona and New Mexico; and in the field fighting Indians, with General Crook, most of the time during the General's stay there.

It was difficult for me to know what to do, and every army woman who has a family of children has gone through this heart struggle; it is so hard to decide just where duty lies. But it was finally decided for me that I should remain with the children, for the boys were too old to take back into a garrison, and I felt they were almost too young to be put at boarding-school for a while. The Colonel left immediately for Fort Lyon, where he joined his squadron and started for Arizona, *via* New Mexico. Colonel Compton was in command until they reached Santa Fé, where he remained with his squadron, and the Colonel with his command marched on to Fort Grant, Arizona; they were three months on the road, but had no trouble with the Indians during the march.

CHAPTER VII.

THE children and I remained with my parents until the following late autumn. I had been on the lookout for a good school to place my lads, and finally decided upon a school in Connecticut, where I took them. In looking back over my life, I think the hardest trial I was called on to bear was leaving those dear boys that dull December afternoon. Dave got his arms about my neck and pleaded with me not to leave him; he said: "I am such a little boy—not eight years old." Jack was a little man and comforter; he swallowed the lump in his throat and said: " Come, Dave, we must take mamma to the carriage; she must not be out late; she has the city to cross." This sobered Dave, for even at that early age they thought they took care of me, as their father left me in their charge. They took me to the carriage. I folded each one to my heart and kissed them again and again, knowing I was going a long distance from them, but never dreaming so many years would pass before I would see them again. I looked back at them as I drove away. The two stood side by side, holding each other's hand. I burst into a flood of tears and wept as I had never wept before in my life.

141

In January, 1876, I started with my little daughter
and nurse for Arizona. We took the express train
for Chicago, there changed cars for Omaha, and thence
to Ogden. The road was not new to me, though it
had greatly improved since I first went over it. A
short stop was made at Ogden for passengers to iden-
tify their luggage and pay for any extra weight
they might have. We were soon off again for San
Francisco, as we supposed our next stop; but the
weather had become very cold, heavy snow was falling, the drifts were great, and we were soon stalled.
The snow-ploughs opened the road over which we
had come to a little frontier town, and our regular
meals, such as they were, were brought to us from
there. Fortunately, I was prepared with some tins
of pâté de fois gras, chicken and deviled ham, also
tea, an alcohol lamp and many other little things
packed by my dear thoughtful mother, whom I think
no emergency ever found unprepared. We were snow-
bound three days before the snow-ploughs succeeded
in digging us out. All this trouble has now been
overcome and the winter is a delightful time to cross
the Continent.

On our arrival in San Francisco we went to the
Occidental Hotel, which has always been frequented
by army people. We remained there the entire winter. Just as the Colonel was starting from Arizona

for me trouble broke out on the Mexican border, and he was ordered out with a squadron to drive back Mexican soldiers from violating neutrality laws; and on his return from that expedition he had to go out after the Chiracauhuas and Apaches, who were under the celebrated Cochise. The character of Arizona at that time was entirely in favor of the Indians, the food consisting of baked mescal-root and other things growing wild in the land they travelled over, so the raids on the white settlers were almost continuous.

While we were waiting for the Colonel I had the pleasure of seeing many of the friends who were so kind to me during that winter when I was there ill and the Colonel at the Modoc War. We also made the acquaintance through Admiral Almy, U. S. N., of a delightful old English gentleman, named William Laird Macgregor. This gentleman belonged to the famous family of ship-builders named Laird in England, but being a second son he had taken his mother's name of Macgregor when he inherited her estate in Scotland. He was well known by all the older officers of our navy, whom he had entertained delightfully at his home in the South of France. He was a great traveller and had been making a tour of our country, intending to return home *via* China; but had been ill and was obliged to wait until he was strong enough for the voyage. He was over seventy years old, but most intellectual and agreeable, also a little eccentric and very systematic, weighing himself before and after each meal; always carried a pedometer or odometer when walking or riding. Broughten, his excellent valet, looked after him as though he were a child. Mr. Macgregor became very fond of my little daughter, who reminded him of a little girl he had lost many years before. He sent to Scotland for pure jams and candies, and many delightful books, which Nellie still has. He was most kind to us both in many ways and we grew very fond of him. Our friendship lasted until his death, many years after, at Arcachon, Gironde, France, where he had built in that lovely climate a white marble palace. For years after we left him, during the time we were in Arizona, he sent English and French papers to us; and, to my astonishment, one day I saw a letter I had written him, descriptive of our journey to Fort Whipple, printed in one of the English papers. He was kind enough to say that Nellie and I had brightened up his enforced stay in San Francisco. I have always believed in the doctrine of compensation. Surely, here was an example. A few years before strangers had ministered unto me and brightened my sick-room, and now here, in the very hotel, I was able to do the same good turn for a stranger.

It was late in March before the Indians were again

144

quiet on their reservations, and the Colonel able to get away and come after us. We had been waiting three months, but the climate was good, the people delightful, and we enjoyed our stay there. We remained but a few days after his arrival, just long enough to buy some extra furniture, carpets, curtains, etc., for the home in Arizona. We said good-bye with great reluctance to our dear old friend, for I felt sure we would never see him again, and when we got to the ship we found he had had my state-room literally covered with flowers, and there were several baskets of most beautiful fruit for our journey. We started one beautiful April morning (such as only California knows in the early spring) on the steamer "Newbern" for Arizona. We ran down the coast with a fair wind and rather close to the shore; I thought I had never seen anything more beautiful. The hills were green and cultivated nearly all the way down. We could see the orange- and lemon-groves in the distance. We were not sick a minute, notwithstanding the old "Newbern" rolled to her heart's content.

There were but few passengers aboard: two or three young officers, going out to join their regiments; Mr. Turner, the agent of the Wells Fargo Express Company, who enjoyed himself hugely playing tricks on me—and I must confess they were clever—and amused the Colonel greatly, who could not always get ahead of me so well. There were also some soldiers and Chinamen. At the mouth of the Colorado River we were transferred in small rowboats to a small steamer, called "The Cocopah," commanded by Captain Polhemus. While the soldiers, Chinamen and freight were getting on board, we watched men in small boats spearing jewfish. It was most interesting. The fish were very large and seemed difficult to reach. Those we took weighed about three hundred pounds, but I was told they often get them weighing over six hundred pounds. They are sometimes caught (and not speared) with a one-hundred-and-eight line, which is the size of an ordinary slate pencil, baited with a large piece of halibut. They were very good tasting, being much like black bass. We took a good many of them with us after they were cut up and packed in ice.

The boat to which we were transferred was a broad, low, flat, stern-wheeler, with an upper deck without a railing around it; the officers and their families and any civilians who might be going to the Territory occupied this part of the boat; soldiers and Chinamen were below. The Colorado, broad, shallow and full of quicksands that are constantly changing, is a remarkable river; it flows through deep cañons in Nevada, the walls of which in some places rise over

146

six thousand feet; it also flows through the Great Cañon, and then through broad, sluggish channels to the sea; the only navigation is along that part of the country where the river separates California and Arizona where we were travelling, the whole country being barren and barbarous. A Cocopah Indian stood at the bow of the boat with a long pole measuring the depth of the water, calling every few moments in measured, monotonous tones its depth, and when it would get too low for the wheels to revolve two men would jump overboard carrying a long heavy chain; they would often go far out of sight, and fastening these chains into rings that were made fast in the rocks, they would wind the boat up to the rings; the chains would be taken off and we would go on. When we came to a particularly large sand-bar the Captain would turn the boat around and the wheel would soon scatter the sand, after which the boat would again be turned and we would creep along. In the night time we were tied up to the banks of the river. One morning the Colonel called me out on the deck to see some Indians on the banks of the river; they were the "Chimehuevis." I was greatly shocked to find the men entirely naked except a piece of cotton which they wore about the loins, and hanging down both front and back; the women wore skirts reaching to the knee; made of leaves; leaving the breasts and legs

147

bare; both men and squaws wore their hair long; they were very dark, tall and most brutal in the expression of their faces. We saw them every day and got accustomed to their nakedness. Sometimes, if the boat was tied up before sundown, they would come aboard, selling fruit or work they had made.

We took twelve days in getting to Fort Yuma, where we remained with Colonel Bradley and his family. It was very, very hot and we slept on enclosed verandas, going to our rooms at sunrise. I so often thought of them afterwards, not only on account of the heat, but because of the lonesomeness of their lives in that God-forsaken country; it must have been very hard for them, yet they bore it uncomplainingly.

It was at Fort Yuma that General Sherman told the story of the old soldier who had been stationed there, died and went to hell. He returned one night and being asked what brought him back, said it was cold, and that he came back for his blankets!

After our boat was unloaded, which took five days, and our cargo put on a smaller boat, we again started up the river. One Sunday night I was singing some hymns, and was surprised to see two Chinamen on the steps leading to our deck. They nodded and smiled, and I asked if they liked the singing. They nodded back and asked if I knew ''Gleenland's Licy

Mountain'' (''Greenland's Icy Mountain''). We all laughed, and I asked them to come near and sing, which they did; it was very funny to hear them. I then asked if they went to Trinity Church Mission; they said no; and I asked if they went to Grace Church Mission; they said no. (I asked because I had friends interested in those Missions in San Francisco.) After awhile one said: ''Me go Baptist to learn Linglish (English). Melican (American) man got heap church and heap Jesus Christ.''

After a short talk with them I found they thought each church, or denomination, had its own Jesus Christ. Another Chinaman I knew asked his mistress one day if she would have an early dinner, which she did. The next day he asked the same favor, when my friend said: ''You had an early dinner yesterday; why do you want it again today?'' He replied: ''Me go to church. Me go last night; preacher he say, me be good boy, me go to heaven, me be angel, me get wings, all same chicken.''

We had a very funny scene just before reaching Ehrenberg. We had a large coop on the deck filled with ducks. In some way a number of them got out and flew overboard. The boat was stopped, two small boats were lowered, and some men went after them. As the men would get near enough to touch them the ducks would dive down, out of sight, and

149

come up at some distance away. It was great fun for us watching, and the soldiers and Chinamen had a good many bets on them. We lost three or four of the ducks, and it was a serious loss in that part of the land, as I afterwards found out.

We reached Ehrenberg just before sundown four days after leaving Fort Yuma. It was only a depot for supplies that were shipped to the forts in all parts of the Territory; and here, entirely isolated from the world, lived Lieutenant and Mrs. Jack Summerhays, with only one other white man—a Mr. Vandevere, the clerk or secretary. They were very glad to see us and gave us the warmest welcome, though we had never before met. We had a very good dinner, notwithstanding it was so far out of the world, for most army women learned to cook and make the best of everything that came within reach. I was somewhat surprised when a very tall, thin Indian in the very garb I have before described came in the dining-room to serve the dinner, which he did quite well. There was much to talk about before I thought of putting my little one to bed, and I asked Mrs. Summerhays if I might have a tub of warm water to give Nelly a bath. In a little while she told me it was ready in my room (which I soon learned was her own she had given up to me). We said good-night, and going to the room I undressed the child and gave

150

her a refreshing bath, the first that she had had since leaving San Francisco. She soon fell asleep and after I had straightened the room a bit, I decided I would get in the tub. I had just sat down in the water when my room door was silently opened and in walked the tall Indian carrying a tray filled with silver before him. I scarcely breathed so great was my fright. He walked over to the table, put the tray down, and as silently walked out, looking neither to the right or the left. It is useless for me to attempt to describe what I felt, it would convey nothing.

The next morning I was sitting at the breakfast-table with my hostess while the Indian cleared the table. She was telling me the great difficulties she had encountered in training the Indian to cook and wait upon them. She had tried several squaws and found them impossible. Often when this man would leave the dining-room to get anything from the kitchen he would remain away so long they would look for him and find him fast asleep on a bench. They never complained; they were glad to see him there, for they never knew what moment he would tire of his work and leave the house not to return, and there was no one else to call upon to help her with the work.

While we were talking Nelly ran in calling, "Mamma, come out and see who is here." I went quickly, and to my great delight and surprise there was Mary Brodcrick, who had lived with me at Fort Lyon. This faithful girl had crossed the plains from Fort Lyon to Arizona with the Colonel and his command, cooking for him and the bachelor officers, never once complaining of the hardships she endured. When she heard the soldiers and escort talking of coming to Ehrenberg to meet us, she insisted upon coming with them to cook for me, saying she would not let me eat soldiers' cooking; and she took that seven days' ride across the desert, sleeping at night rolled in a blanket on the ground under the stars. I was greatly touched by her devotion.

At about 8.30 A.M. we were ready to move. The luggage was stowed in the great army waggons, and the things for use on the road were in a smaller one. The ambulance, with four shining mules, and driver with his long whip in hand, was ready to start. It took a few moments to say "good-bye" to these delightful people—whom I always thought should have a medal for their services there, protecting the supplies that came into the Territory for the officers and soldiers, entirely surrounded by hostile Indians, and not much more than a corporal's guard to depend on aside from some Indian scouts.

The country through which we rode was dry, sandy and sterile; the glare of light was so great that the sand-plains glowed beneath the glowing sun, and we travelled slowly. At mid-day we stopped for luncheon by what seemed to me the bottom of a creek, but the men dug down and found a little spring. The heat was intense. One could scarcely breathe. The very crows sat drooping and open-mouthed, too hot to caw, but when disturbed sailed through the brazen sky without seeming effort.

At two o'clock we were off again. There was no change in the character of the country; we could see for miles in every direction, the mountains looming in the distance. Toward night-fall it became a little cooler, and we camped near a small stream.

We had a complete camping outfit, which included a tent and some bed-springs on which to lay my mattress and pillow. Everything was as comfortable as possible, considering we were crossing a desert; Nellie and Mary were with me in the tent, while the Colonel slept on the ground near the men and close to my tent door, and although I knew I was in a country where the Indians were warlike I never had a calmer sleep than my first night on this great desert. I had great confidence in the soldiers of the Sixth Cavalry (who were there for my protection) who had fought so many hard fights against these Apaches, and no fear had yet entered my heart; alas, it was to come later. In the morning we were up early; it was

most beautiful, and as far as the eye could reach not
a sign of life could be seen; we seemed to be the only
living people on the planet. After dressing my little
girl we went out to see Mary get breakfast. She had
become an old campaigner and went about her work
as though in her own kitchen; we had a fine mess
chest, and a dutch oven in which the bread and biscuit were baked. We also had an arrangement made
of wire to put meat or game on to broil; the Colonel
shot plenty for all of us, including escort, teamsters
and ourselves. The out-door life was delightful; the
desert seemed a wonderful place to me; already I was
beginning to feel its atmosphere and no longer wondered at the gypsies. Nelly was as happy as a bird,
and as well as possible. Soon after breakfast we
broke camp, and at eight o'clock were off for the
day's march. The road was lined with cactus of
every description, wonderful and beautiful to me,
as the plains of neither Nevada or Colorado have this
beautiful plant. There were also the mesquite trees,
a species of acacia which grow to the height of ten
or twelve feet; the seeds, which are contained in a
small pod, are used by the Indians to make bread; it
is quite sweet, palatable and very nutritious. The
wood of these trees is very hard and heavy. They
were almost the only trees we saw excepting the willows which grow by the little streams and springs

154

and where you generally find a ranch. When we stopped for luncheon one of the teamsters told me a story of a massacre that had occurred almost at the very spot where we had camped: ''One day a large party of Apaches swooped down upon a ranch occupied by some Mexicans; the men fled, leaving the women and children to their fate. Those who were not carried away were violated and pierced with arrows and left for dead. The ranchero's wife with two grown daughters fled before the Indians reached the house and hid themselves under a wooden bridge a few feet away from where we stood. After a while, some Indians, including a chief, came to the bridge, and catching sight of the women, stood for some little time talking, saying what they would do when they caught them. The poor women were frightened almost senseless; suddenly the Indians jumped from the bridge with a savage yell and thrust a knife into the woman. The chief seized the elder girl, saying he would take her for his wife. He put her on a pony, and mounting another, they all rushed toward the mountain. After some time the mother and daughter ventured to go from their hiding-place. The poor creatures found their home plundered and the dead bodies of their friends and relatives on the ground.''

This story was not calculated to relieve any fear

155

I might have and though it had occurred many years before I was glad to start off again leaving the scene of this frightful massacre behind me. We had not stopped long for luncheon. As we had a mountain to cross which was very steep, the Colonel, Nelly and Mary got out of the ambulance and walked quite a distance and the escort dismounted and led their horses, which were slowly walked. On reaching the summit the scene was entrancing. The mountains stretched away on each side, and some isolated peaks stood out in bold relief. We could see a stream winding its way through a cañon; we stopped for a few minutes only, as we had still a long distance to ride before reaching water, but the silent picture will ever remain in my mind, as will the wonderful sunset we saw that evening. We were still high in the mountain, the horizon seemed to be a wonderful lake; every moment it seemed as though we would drive into it; as I looked from the ambulance it appeared to be not a hundred yards away. At first the colour of this lake looked crimson, with great streaks of silver gray, blue, and a golden reddish brown, like varnished copper; then there were great stretches of violet. Gradually the sky became more silvery, with wonderful fleecy clouds of blue in several tones, and the golden reddish brown was in great waves which looked like wings and one great hand spread as if in a bless-

ing. All along the horizon were beautiful silvery
clouds with white patches that looked like snow, and
as if a great light in all colours was thrown on it.
Sometimes it seemed as though we were above it. It
lasted fully an hour. We were going down the mountain directly towards the west. I feel I cannot
describe it, nor can I describe my feelings as I watched
it. Never before had I realised how greatly colour
could affect me; it seemed as though the heavenly
gates were open and I was having a glimpse of the
New Jerusalem.

We camped near a little stream. Nelly and I
watched the men caring for the mules, and then getting their supper. They seemed very happy and not
to mind the lonesomeness. It was the stillness that
impressed me. There were no birds, and only an
occasional crow to be seen near where we were camped.

The next morning we made an early start; crossed
the desert until we came to a mountain that rose
abruptly from the plain and was crested with a wall
some two hundred feet high and was nearly perpendicular, forming one of the noted landmarks of the
country. High mesas (mountains that have flat tops)
closed in here and formed a cañon through which we
rode. The trail was narrow, barely six feet wide. The
mountain towered above us on our right, and a deep
precipice was on our left. It was very weird and

made me feel strangely as we crawled along, for the ascent was difficult. There was not a sound, only the tread of the mules and the horses which the soldiers rode; not even a sound of insect life could be heard. The stillness was of death; the tension terrible. It was called the ''Dead Man's Cañon,'' not only because of the massacres that had occurred there, but also because of the entire absence of life, insect as well as animal. At about four o'clock we drove rapidly down the cañon and turned into a beautiful valley. Here were hundreds of cacti in bloom—red, purple, yellow, and white. I uttered a psalm of thanksgiving, the sight was so beautiful, and coming as it did so unexpectedly upon me thrilled me, and it was with difficulty that I controlled my feelings.

After a short drive through this beautiful valley we came to the spot where we camped near the profile of Montezuma; and as we drove in at sundown and approached the mountain, old Montezuma's face loomed through the deepening twilight clearly outlined against the western sky, gradually growing plainer as we approached, until it seemed a fully formed colossal image with arms folded on its breast and shrouded in the cerements of the tomb. It was so majestic, rising as it did from the solemn plains, it filled me with awe, and I quietly sat gazing at it until the sun had gone and the red and yellow light was

158

fast disappearing, so that it was too dark for me to
see, and I went into my tent to think over the day,
which seemed to me the most wonderful of my life.

The next day we passed the scene of another massacre, which had also occurred two years before. A
whole family were killed, excepting two young girls,
who were taken captives by the Apaches. We saw the
graves where those who were killed were buried by
some passers-by. It depressed me greatly; and though
the tragedy had occurred some time before, it dwelt in
my mind, and as we drove on I could not help wondering what the lives of the two captive girls had been.

The country through which we travelled the morning of the third day was rolling, and there was a fine
stream by which we stopped for an early luncheon.
The Colonel as usual had killed plenty of game as it
abounded near the streams. That afternoon we had
a long march across the desert to get water for the
night's camp, so we did not rest long, but started off
and rode quickly to cross the long stretch of desert
before night-time should overtake us. Just before
sundown two of the escort, one leading the Colonel's
horse, rode rapidly back to the ambulance to speak
to the Colonel, who was riding with me. He immediately got down to talk with them, and I knew it was
about something serious. Whenever the Colonel rode
with me, he had his rifle ready for instant use, as

all of the escort had, but before riding off with the men, he took a pistol from its case and while hurriedly loading it, said: " The men see signs of Indians; I must ride ahead for a while." He handed me the pistol saying: "Keep courage and remember what I have always told you—never let an Indian take you alive." A great lump rose in my throat; my head swam, and I was terribly scared, but almost instantly I thought of my child who must be protected; and the poor girl who had braved danger in coming to make my journey across the desert more comfortable was in a panic of fear, so in trying to reassure her my own courage was somewhat restored. We rode very slowly on, each one filled with his own thoughts; ten minutes seemed an hour, and the sun was fast sinking in the western sky. Each moment I thought I could bear the suspense no longer. We stopped, and it seemed an eternity before the Colonel returned, but I saw from his face, before he spoke, that he was somewhat relieved. He said: "There are signs of Indians, but I think they have passed on, and we will go on as rapidly as possible," which we did, the escort remaining very close. That night we camped at a stage station, which we reached about nine o'clock. The Colonel asked if I would rather go in, and sleep in the house, but I preferred the tent, with the soldiers all around; but there was not much sleep for me.

The next morning we broke camp early; it was much cooler, and the country more settled. We passed several ranches and had a pleasant but uneventful day, the only thing of particular interest being the passing of the stage coach with the four horses on a run, carrying the mail; it was the only team of any kind we had seen since leaving Ehrenberg. That night was our last camping station. We had a fine supper of biscuit, coffee, game, and potatoes. The moon came out bright (and it seems to be brighter and to give a softer light in that wonderful climate than anywhere else) and we sat long by the camp-fire, talking and singing.

Next morning we were off bright and early. We hoped to reach Prescott by two o'clock, and although I had enjoyed the outdoor life, and the wonderful country I had gone over, I was glad to reach our destination; but my little girl and the Colonel would gladly have kept on, notwithstanding it was thirty days since we had left San Francisco. He loved the out-door life and the shooting, and the little one was all unconscious of fear.

When we were within a few miles of Prescott, on a hill overlooking the town, I was thinking of the long journey, and how far away I was from the two dear lads at school. I almost broke down; but the Colonel, seeing what was in my mind, called my attention to a beautiful garden, which he knew I loved. I looked at it, but could not speak; and during the long years I lived at Fort Whipple I never drove past that garden, no matter how gay the party was that I was with, without feeling that same emotion I felt the first morning I saw it.

We had to drive through Prescott, the capital of the Territory, to reach Fort Whipple. It was a small but well-built town. There was a plaza, or park, in the center of the town and stores on the four sides of it. One side was given up to the saloons; but it was fairly orderly, considering it was a mining town. There was a good element from the beginning, and disorderly people were not allowed to remain long. I never saw a place grow so rapidly and improve in every way as it did during the five and a half years we lived near it. There was an excellent society—lawyers, mining engineers, and their families, and other business men; also a great number of miners.

CHAPTER VIII.

On reaching the fort we drove to Lieutenant Anderson's quarters. He had telegraphed us when we were at Fort Yuma, asking us to be his guests; and although the General in command and others had been equally kind, we thought best to go to our old friend. Such a welcome as we had! I had hardly gotten the dust from my face and hands when General and Mrs. Kautz were announced, and soon after all of the staff officers and their wives and many others from the garrison. Champagne was opened and our health and hearty welcome drunk. The whole afternoon was spent in going over old Indian fights and campaigns, for here were officers who had served through the Modoc, Sioux, Arapaho, Apache and other Indian wars. Stories were told of thrilling escapes and I, not yet recovered from the fright of a few nights before, told of our alarm. They said the Indians were off their reservation committing depredations, and that a troop had gone out early the morning before, and if we had not arrived by three o'clock some troops would have been sent out to look for us. So we really made a lucky escape. It was supposed

163

the Indians thought we had a larger force than we had, seeing so many waggons.

Fort Whipple was the headquarters of the Department of Arizona. It was situated about one mile from the town of Prescott, which had been established as close to the fort as possible on account of the Indians. There was a good stream of water running through the garrison and some small willows and cottonwood trees, making quite an oasis in the desert. The quarters for the officers and their families were poor and unattractive. General Kautz, the colonel of the Eighth Infantry, then stationed there, was in command of the Department. He was a fine soldier and a man of great integrity; loved not only by the officers and soldiers, but by every one in the Territory. The staff officers all lived on a sloping hill overlooking the garrison, and huge granite mountains were in the distance. Directly facing the house we occupied, but miles away, was a huge mountain of rock towering above all others, called "Thumb Butte," as it was in the shape of a hand doubled with the thumb up.

The staff officers' quarters were better (because newer) than those of the garrison, but there were but two sets that could really be called good. They were all built alike,—low, broad houses with hall in the center, and two rooms about sixteen feet square on

each side; pantry and kitchen back, also an attic above.
I often looked through the cracks in my house to
the light outside. They were built of wood and ceiled
(as there was no plaster to be had), and in that dry
climate the wood shrunk, leaving great slits for the
light and air to come in, and as there was often in
winter a difference of fifty degrees in temperature
between the day and night-time, we had to keep great
fires going continually. We had no stoves or fur-
naces; only the large open hearth fire, and it is needless to say it was hard at times to keep warm. We
bought thin muslin, something like cheese-cloth, and
had it tacked over the walls of the living-room, and
bed-room and papered them, the muslin holding the
paper, a soft gray ground with the passion vine and
red flower in full bloom. We had sent to San Francisco for it, and it took just four months to reach
us after the order was sent. The Government at that
time allowed no extra money to make the quarters
comfortable, and I doubt if many of the discomforts
we had were realised at Washington.

We were so far from the railway that when officers
came from a distance we were so glad to see and to
talk with them about what was going on in the world,
that our discomforts were for a time forgotten.

We were not long in getting settled. An officer
and his family were in the quarters we were entitled

to, but as they were expecting to go East soon we made ourselves comfortable for the time in a small house. The Colonel was now on duty as Inspector General of the Department, and was on General Kautz's staff. There were some delightful people at Fort Whipple, among them Colonel and Mrs. Wilkins, whom I had not seen since we left Macon, Georgia, and their beautiful daughter Miss Carrie, whom every officer fell in love with in less than twenty-four hours after his arrival, and it was the same when she went to visit a garrison. All the youngsters fell down before her. Colonel Jim Martin was the Adjutant General of the Department, and I suppose a more competent adjutant general, or more congenial man, was never in the army. His wife was very beautiful. Colonel Rodney Smith was there, with his bride. Colonel Chandler, a bachelor at that time, most agreeable and with a fine war record; Dr. Magruder and his wife and daughters; Captain Simpson and his wife, and dear little Amy with her beautiful hair like spun gold; Lieutenant Earl D. Thomas and his interesting wife and three little girls; besides a great many others.

It was a very gay post, with an entertainment of some kind almost every day and evening. In fact years after we used to allude to the time when General Kautz was in command, as ''the days of the

Empire.'' The officers were going scouting continually, so there was no time for the routine there now
is in the army. Soldiers learned from actual experience in the hardest kind of warfare, and strange
to say there were fewer desertions. When the officers
had their turn to remain in the garrison it was pretty
lively with dinners, dances, and the rehearsals of
plays, for we had a most excellent Dramatic Society,
and presented some very good plays every winter.
I have been at a ''hop,'' and once at a play, when
we heard the ''Assembly Call.'' Every officer
dropped his partner and ran to his troop, and in an
hour's time they were in the saddle and off to catch
the Apaches, who were on the war-path, killing and
destroying everything they passed. Although the
Colonel was on detached duty from his regiment as
Inspector General, he never let his men go out on these
expeditions without going with them if possible. We
generally had a little something for them to eat at
our house before they left, and a sandwich to go in
their pockets; for often they had an all-night ride,
and sometimes longer, before they could stop for
anything.

The days for the women were all alike. Usually
in the morning we rode or drove, and we sewed a part
of every day and ofttimes in the evenings, for as I
have said we had all our own and our children's

clothes to make, besides the adornment of our houses. I remember very well upholstering a lounge and two chairs in pretty light blue cretonne with apple blossoms on it. A soldier in Lieutenant Kingsbury's troop made the frames out of some boxes we had, and he tied in some springs that I was able to get in town, and I did the rest of the work. I also made window-curtains of the same material with fluted swiss ruffles, and lined with a soft unbleached cotton. They were very pretty and when they were drawn at night to keep out the cold, our room was charmingly pretty and cosy. Years after an officer told me there was not (to his mind) as pretty a room in Washington as my dainty little living-room on the frontier. This showed how little of the beautiful we had around us. In fact we would have been starved had it not been for the blue skies, the wonderful rugged mountains, and the mystery of the desert.

I remember one occasion shortly after our arrival at Fort Whipple. There was a great outbreak of the Indians in the Territory. All the troops of the command were ordered out except enough to protect the garrison. The Colonel was away on an inspecting tour, and General Kautz, who was always thoughtful of others, came and insisted upon Nellie and myself going to his house in the garrison to remain during the excitement. We had been there but a few days when the outbreak became so general and the excitement in the Territory so great that General Kautz and all of his staff went to the southern part of the Territory to be on hand in case they were needed, as the General would there be nearer the scene of action. I remained with Mrs. Kautz until the return of the troops and greatly enjoyed her hospitality, as she was a charming hostess.

In the month of June eighteen hundred and seventy-seven we had a son born to us, christened James Harwood, for my great-grandfather. I had been unable to secure a nurse; such a luxury was not then to be had in that part of the country. I was very ill and my child frail and delicate. Dear Mrs. Wilkins, whom I had known in Macon, Georgia, whose husband was the lieutenant-colonel of the Eighth Infantry now stationed at "Whipple," came every morning, gave my little son his bath, dressed him, and did everything for us both, that her generous heart dictated, but my child staid with us only three short weeks. I wept so much seeing his struggles for breath, knowing he was suffering, that trouble came upon my eyes and I was kept in a darkened room. Dr. McKey and Dr. Worthington both feared cataract, but after six weeks the disease yielded to treatment. All of the officers and ladies came during the time doing all they could to cheer me. General and Mrs.

Kautz lost their little daughter under almost the same conditions that had cost my child's life.

The following autumn three Sisters of Charity, including Mother Monica, of whom we became so fond, came to Prescott to establish a much-needed hospital, and I went down to see them and ask in what way I could help them, for they had really nothing to begin on. Every one in the place was interested, for it was a fine charity and much needed. When the poor miners in the vicinity met with an accident or were ill there had been no place for them to go for treatment. The officers and ladies at the fort gave a play, "The Two Orphans," charging a dollar admission. The little room was so crowded we were almost scared, and I would give much if I had a photograph of the audience. There were all classes and conditions of men, but all well-behaved and appreciative. We raised considerable money, and added to the amount the good sisters raised in the town and county they were able almost immediately to build the hospital, as the merchants promised generous contributions monthly for its support. Brave, hearty, generous frontiersmen, who does not admire them? I think I must tell that a few gentlemen in town had a game of poker once or twice a week, and when the Colonel was not off on his inspecting tours he used to go down and play with them, though it was a rule of his life while in the service never to play cards when in command of a garrison. One day he stopped at the hospital to see how they were getting along. Some conversation took place about "the game" in town, when the Colonel promised that whenever he made a winning he would stop by and divide with them for the benefit of the hospital, which he did; but some time later when I was there Mother Monica asked: "What has become of the Colonel? We have not seen him for a long time." "Ah! well, then, Mother," I said, "he can't have been winning." While talking of the hospital I think I must tell of an incident that further strengthened my belief in the doctrine of compensation. A few years after we had left Fort Whipple an uncle of mine went to Prescott to look after some mining property. When within a mile of the city, going down the steep hill I have referred to before, some part of the harness broke; the horses ran, throwing the coach over an embankment; my uncle was picked up and carried to the hospital and found to be seriously injured. On his return to consciousness some time later, he inquired for Colonel Biddle, thinking he might be at the garrison. When the sisters learned he was a relative of ours they could not do enough for him, and they nursed him so carefully his life was saved to his family.

At this time there was a very estimable lady living

171

in the garrison, a veritable Mrs. Malaprop. She told us of some jewelry she had lost, and among the things was a topaz chain with a beautiful "pendulum." One Friday evening we went to the hop-room for the usual dance. It had been newly painted, and Miss Wilkins remarked that the odour was not pleasant, when the lady, who was present, said: "Oh! dear, new paint always did make me nauseous." She also told us she had several "relicts" of the Revolution, and she was heard telling a stranger that we had to "irritate" the soil in Arizona to raise crops. Her husband died suddenly and the doctor asked: "Did your husband speak before he died?" "Oh, no!" she said, "he just gave three grasps and died."

Whenever an officer left the Territory it was the practice to have an auction, selling off everything he did not care to keep—even to his clothes sometimes, as they had generally been in the Territory some years and the civilian clothes brought in would not do very well after getting back to the States. The lady I refer to held an auction before leaving, and when some silver-plated knives were put up for sale, she rose, and in a sobbing voice said: "Oh, dear, no! I cannot sell them; they have been in dear John's mouth too often."

These auctions were a great institution. They enabled the settlers to buy furniture and other things

at a fair price. Freighting was enormously high—
twelve and one half cents per pound when we went
into the Territory, and it had been higher. The
ladies and officers always attended because it meant a
frolic, and besides we always bought something.
When we first went into the Territory I should have
been delighted to have attended an auction, as I did
later, for I had to pay $7 for a washtub, $2 apiece
for flat-irons, $2 per pound for butter, $2 a dozen for
eggs, and so on. A cook could not be gotten under
$50 per month, and a housemaid $25, and everything
was proportionately high. I often wondered how the
young lieutenants lived on their pay. Perhaps I
might give a couple of recipes that we used, showing
how one can get along without either milk or eggs.

Custard without eggs or milk: Six tablespoonfuls
of cornstarch; enough water to make it creamy thick
when cooked; add essence of lemon and sugar to taste;
serve in custard-cups.

Apple-pie, without apples: Soda crackers soaked
in water, and warmed until soft, but do not break too
fine; add essence of lemon and sugar and a great deal
of nutmeg; bake in pastry, with a top crust to the pie.

You will feel sure it is apple-pie (if you do not
make it yourself). These recipes were handed down
from Mrs. Coolidge, who was on the frontier in 1850,
and knew more privations than we did; but she is

still living and is a most charming old lady, full of anecdote and interest. I had not been long at Fort Whipple before I bought from a lady, the wife of Judge Lieb who had a ranch near, a setting of good eggs, for which I paid $3, and she lent me a hen that wanted to set and I began to raise chickens and turkeys. I sold over two hundred of the former and fourteen of the latter, besides having all we wanted and plenty of both eggs and chickens to give away. We also bought a cow from a man who was driving a herd up from Texas. Poor fellow, he had lost many, and was glad to sell out what remained at Prescott. We sold three cows at our auction, and I had had the pleasure of sending milk every day to both hospitals, the one at the fort for the soldiers, and the one in town erected while we lived at "Whipple."

I remember some years later, when Colonel Martin got his orders to go East, he held the usual auction. That morning the Colonel said to me, "Don't go to that auction to-day. We have already so much stuff we shall never get rid of it." About eleven o'clock I was sitting sewing when I heard some people run hastily up our steps and in a moment Lieutenant Kingsbury, Lieutenant Evans and Lieutenant Willcox appeared saying, "Mr. Fisher, the auctioneer, is waiting for you; no one will bid; all expect you to

open the auction,'' as I usually did. Off I went.
They were in the kitchen and when I got there Mr.
Fisher, seeing me, put up a chopping-bowl with
chopper, kitchen knives and some long-handled spoons
and other little things. No one bid, so just to start
it I said, ''Twenty-five cents;'' no one bid against me
and the things were knocked down to me. The
officers and ladies roared with laughter, for just as
they were handed over to me in walked the Colonel,
and all knew the orders I had received in the morning.
However, it started the auction and all went well;
we carried the things home and I told the Chinaman
to put them on the top shelf of the pantry and not
to use them. They were afterwards sold at our
auction separately for one dollar and fifty cents.

I have almost forgotten to tell about my good Mary
Broderick, the maid we took from Junction City. We
had been at Fort Whipple about two years when she
was married to a Mr. Stephenson, who was the chief
clerk of the Department, a clever, highly educated
man, evidently belonging to a good family in Scotland, from which country he came. He had been in-
temperate and I was afraid to let Mary marry him,
but when he asked my consent I told him he could
have Mary when he proved to me that he could stop
drinking and provide a home for her. I had taken this
girl from her family and friends and felt my respon-

175

sibility was great. At the end of a year the home was provided and he had stopped drinking, so they were married in our parlour, General Kautz, Colonel Martin, and my husband signing the register. I regret to say my fears were not groundless for, after about three years of married life, disappointed at not having a son born to them he began to drink again. He lost his position and they moved to Colorado, where I lost sight of them, much to my regret. Many years after we learned, through his family trying to find him, that he had been disinherited, but had they had a son, he (the son) would have inherited a large estate in Scotland.

In September, 1878, we had a visit from General Sherman and two of his staff officers, who came on a tour of inspection. General and Mrs. Kautz and the Eighth Infantry had been ordered to California, and General Orlando Willcox with the Twelfth Infantry had taken their places. General Willcox was in command of the Department. I had known him many years—in fact, he was one of a few officers present at our wedding. He was a handsome, genial man, with a fine war record, commanding for a time in the Ninth Army Corps. As soon as I heard the General of the Army was coming I wrote to Lieutenant Kingsbury and Lieutenant Baird asking them to send me some game, and a fish, if possible, from the Verde River, as I wanted to give the General a dinner. I received a note in reply telling me, that some men would go the next day for the game, and that I should have the fish if they had to blow the river up to get it for me. Of course I took this as extravagant talk; however, in a few days a cart came from Verde (forty miles) filled with game of all kinds,—wild turkeys, ducks, quail, etc., etc., and there were two fine big fish, which delighted me greatly; there was also a note telling me there had been difficulty in getting the fish, and that "the creatures" had very ugly heads, but they thought I could dress them up with parsley, etc., and they would look well. The day after the arrival of the cart we heard that some one had thrown a dynamite cartridge in the Verde River and a number of fish had been killed. This was a serious matter, and I was a bit scared, but said nothing; the Colonel was the Inspector General of the Department, and if he had known I was the cause none of us would have been spared.

I was greatly pleased to see the General. He and my dear father had been friends for many years before the war, and the Colonel had belonged to General Sherman's army, but left it at Atlanta, Georgia, with General Stoneman's cavalry, of which the Colonel commanded a brigade. I so well remember the informal reception given the General by General

Willcox the first evening of his arrival. All of the
officers and their wives, as well as all of the bachelor
officers, were asked to meet him. When I was presented he took my hand, saying in his hearty manner,
"Why, my child, I knew your father in California
in eighteen hundred and fifty, in the stirring times,
and if memory serves me right, your brother-in-law
Harmony was there also, and I have known them ever
since." He had a chair placed beside him for me
to sit down, and playfully added, "Don't run away
with these youngsters," who were standing by ready
to ask me to dance. I felt quite like a queen (for I
was always a hero-worshipper), and never was prouder
in my life; it seemed to me a great thing to have
this great man make much of me. The evening came
for our dinner to the General and it was very good.
I had a most excellent Chinaman cook named
"Flang," quite young, and he always dressed in very
pretty Chinese coats, and, to match the costume, a hat
that had a tassel on, which he had a peculiar little
way of throwing one side. The General was much
surprised to see fish in that part of the world and
spoke of it, and I held my breath lest some one should
speak of the blowing up of the river. It was delightful to listen to the conversation of these men. They
realised how greatly we were cut off from the world
and told us everything they could think of to interest

178

us, even to the little Washington gossip, so dear to a woman's heart. There were twelve officers and eight ladies, including Mrs. Richard Wainwright (wife of Captain Wainwright, U. S. N., who has so greatly distinguished himself since). She and her little daughter were visiting her brother, Lieutenant Wotherspoon, and she added greatly to the pleasure of the garrison, having travelled a great deal, and aside from her good memory she had a charming way of telling things. When the dessert was brought in I had a great fright. A large fish was presented to me. "Oh! my," I thought, "has he cooked another fish?" My heart was beating very fast, when some one said, "Did you ever see anything so perfect?" It was a Charlotte Russe; the Chinaman had imitated the fish, and it was perfect, greatly to my relief.

The citizens of Prescott gave the General a reception. He had been there many years before, and all of the old "Hassyamps" flocked to see him again. General Willcox and the General asked me to receive with them, and as I stood beside General Sherman I mentioned each one's name quietly as they approached him. I knew every one in the country and although the General knew the faces of all he had met, I feared, seeing so many, he might not be able to recall their names and I gave him no chance to forget, while the old rough but kindly men were glad to be remembered. The General gave me at this time an auto-graph picture of himself, which I have always greatly prized.

We often rode over to Fort Verde for a dinner or dance, and to visit Captain and Mrs. Wallace. We usually left Fort Whipple about eight o'clock A.M., and when we started it was telegraphed to Verde; if we did not arrive on time, a sergeant and some men would come flying out to look us up, the Indians being bad in that locality. I recollect, with great pleasure, one trip we made. We drove a few miles beyond "Verde" to see Montezuma's well. It was a very remarkable place, about one hundred and fifty feet in diameter and fifty feet deep. At the sides of this well were caves resembling houses leading far in under the mountain, with great subterranean pas-sages. We started to explore them, but there were so many turns it was decided best not to go too far. We found several interesting pieces of pottery, arrow-heads, and other curious things. It is said this great well could be flooded. I have since understood that this cave has been explored and houses, much like those used by the Aztecs, found; also many curious Indian relics. I forgot to mention a young Indian boy, about nineteen or twenty years old, who lived with us. He was an Apache and had been left on the field in a fight years before when a small child. The

GENERAL W. T. SHERMAN, U.S.A.

soldiers of the Sixth Cavalry took him and he staid with the troop until he was fourteen years old, when he went to live with Lieutenant Perrine and Lieutenant Kingsbury as their valet. When these officers were departing for the East some years later they wrote to me, asking if I would like to have him, and we decided it would be well to do so. He arrived one evening at nightfall. Colonel took the youth to the kitchen to get his dinner and showed him the room that had been prepared for his occupancy. The next morning I saw the lad for the first time. He was tall and slender, not very dark, with quite a good expression of countenance. I showed him how to wait on the table and how I wished him to wash the dishes and to do the other dining-room work, and then told him when he had finished the room to go to the Colonel's office and the Colonel would take him to town and fit him out with clothes. I then went into the sitting-room, and as it was cool I shut the door leading into the hall. A little later when I was sitting alone sewing I thought I heard the latch turn, but on looking up I saw no one and resumed my work, but presently the door quietly opened and in walked the Indian. "You must not come in here," I said, quickly. "Go down to the Colonel's office." He paid not the slightest attention to me, but picked up a chair and placed it directly in front of me, saying, as he sat down, "I like you much," which did not reassure me. I was really very much frightened, but I did not wish him to know it. So I pushed back my chair and rose, saying, "Come, Charlie (that was the name he had chosen), you must go to the Colonel." He then rose and I walked behind him to the hall, when I opened the front door and quickly slamming it after me, ran down to my husband's office, thoroughly frightened. The lad was soon taught that he must not enter any room where I was without permission, and although he seemed docile and fond of us I was never quite at ease when alone with him. His greatest pleasure was playing marbles. Every day I taught him and he was learning to read quite well. He had been with us for over a year and seemed very happy and content, when Lieutenant Hanna came to Fort Whipple with his enlisted scouts of Pimas and other Indians, which the Government was using against the Apaches. Charlie seemed much depressed and discontented. The Colonel asked him if he wanted to enlist as a scout. He brightened up and said he did. We talked over the matter and decided it was best to let him go for three months, and he would find how hard the life was and would be glad to get back and be more content. He put all of his clothes carefully away in his room and went down to the garrison and enlisted. A few evenings after Nelly came to my room and told me an Indian wanted to see me in the kitchen. I went out and found three braves, and to my surprise one was Charlie, and his face was painted and his hair was matted with mud; a blanket was around his shoulders, and he had on an old pair of soldier's trousers. He was just as much Indian as the others, who had never lived in a house or been with civilised people. Lieutenant Hanna afterwards told me that he was the worst scout he had, and he ran away with two or three other worthless Indians. Since then I have never thought the plan of sending Indian boys to the schools in the East to educate them, and then allow them to go back to their reservations, a good one. There are too many generations of Indians back of them, and the few years of civilisation are soon forgotten.

In the winter of 1879 another son was born to us. He, too, was very delicate; the valve of his heart had not closed and he had great difficulty in breathing. We were fortunate in having Dr. Ainsworth with us, who was a master in his profession; and although he has since proven himself so efficient in the Record and Pension Bureau, it seems a pity that he should have given up the highest profession—that of saving life—in which he was so eminently successful. He watched my babe so carefully, doing everything for him that science had made known, that each day we saw the little life grow stronger, and we have never forgotten that we owe the lad's life to his watchful care. I had an excellent nurse, a Mrs. Bailey. My husband had sent to San Francisco for her, not only paying her expenses to come to us, but gave her one hundred dollars per month from the date she started. She remained with us three months, then went to some ladies in the garrison who needed her services. Some time afterwards I sent for her to come to see me. After telling her when I would again need her, I said, "You are certainly not going to charge me as much as before, especially as you have been constantly occupied and are doing so well." The old lady dropped her head and thought awhile, then said, "Well, madam, if you are going to make a yearly job of this, I guess I can come for ninety dollars per month." She saw nothing funny in this, but I did not engage her at the discount.

An amusing incident occurred about this time. A young officer in the garrison was too fond of going to the sutler's to throw dice for drinks. He had a lovely wife and babe, and he was persuaded to "go on the water waggon," as the men said whenever they stopped drinking. I think I have said that army officers make excellent husbands; they are always ready to help their wives in every way they can. One day this young fellow found his wife very busy, and

said, "If you will put the little one in its carriage I
will run her up and down the board-walk." The
babe was soon tenderly tucked in the carriage, and
the proud young father pushed the carriage some
time. At one end of the board-walk was the sutler's,
and finally the temptation got too great and he rolled
the carriage round to the back door and ran in to get
a glass of beer. Two young second lieutenants seeing
him place the carriage so carefully out of sight,
thought they would have some fun. One took the
baby out of the carriage and ran out of sight, while
the other put a log of wood in its place and covered
it up very carefully. By and by the proud father
came out and started home, calling his wife when he
reached there to come get the child. She threw back
the pretty blankets and there lay the log of wood!
She looked at her husband and demanded to know
"what he had done with the child." He declared he
had done nothing with the child, that the carriage
was just as she had fixed it, whereupon the wife went
into hysterics and the whole garrison was aroused.
The culprits, finding the trouble they had caused,
speedily returned the babe, much to the chagrin of
the officer whose little secret was learned.

And here I must tell a funny story on myself.
One day the Colonel seeing Nick playing in the dirt
dressed prettily in white, which he knew I had spent

much time in making, said rather positively, ''Don't buy another inch of that abominable trimming stuff for that child; get something more suitable, some colored material.'' So the next day I drove down to Goldwater's store to get some brown and blue linen, if possible. As I entered the store Mr. Morris Goldwater approached me, saying, ''We have just received some of the handsomest embroideries we have ever had.'' ''I cannot buy any more,'' I replied. ''Colonel says he won't pay for another inch. I am to buy dark linens.'' ''Well! you can look at them,'' he said, which I did, and wanted some very much, but I knew the Colonel was right and said no, Colonel would not like it. He replied, ''Why not call it something else,—sundries, lamp chimneys, anything? The Colonel don't mind what you buy.'' It struck me as a very funny idea and I took several yards and forgot all about the incident as soon as I left the shop. At the end of every month the Colonel always brought me the bills, telling me to look over them and see if they were correct before he paid them. The first I took up was Goldwater's, and the first thing that struck my eyes was the number of lamp chimneys charged. (We always used a great many, as the changes in temperature were so great they would crack during the day as well as when used.) I cried out, ''What do you suppose he means by putting so

186

many lamp chimneys on the bill? We could not have gotten them." "Well, you had better drive down and see about it," said the Colonel, and that afternoon we went. I walked in the store and said, "Why, Mr. Goldwater, you have put all of the lamp chimneys used in the garrison this month on my bill." He looked rather curious and then suggested, "Perhaps the man got them." "Well, if he did," I replied, "you should have known better than to have given him such a quantity without an order." Just then the Colonel walked off, saying, "You two must settle it yourselves," when Mr. Goldwater quietly remarked, "Did you forget the embroidery we called 'lamp chimneys'?" I nearly swooned with laughter, and calling the Colonel told him all about it; the joke was too good to keep and you may know he was delighted to have it, and told it very often in after years. It all reminded me of my childhood; when I got into any particular mischief my dear mother would ask no questions but say to my older sisters, "Just give her rope enough and she will hang herself," for somehow it would always come out.

In those days I played the guitar and sang all the old-fashioned songs, which I had heard my dear mother sing when I was a child. Some of them were "Mary of Argyle," "When stars were in the quiet skies," "Believe me if all those endearing young charms,'' and many others. Each officer had his favourite song, and several of them went to the bandmaster and learned to tune the guitar. They would come in, take up the guitar, tune it, and hand it to me. I always knew which song to sing. That dear old Martin guitar is still giving pleasure. My eldest son plays delightfully upon it, and often upon a summer night while he plays I sing the same old songs to the dear children, who have brought so much happiness into my life, and memory carries me back to the days spent on the desert.

I was greatly surprised one morning to receive a letter from my brother, Paymaster McGowan, United States Navy, telling me he soon expected to be relieved from the Pacific Squadron and ordered East, and if I would send Nelly to San Francisco he would take her with him. I had felt for some time I would soon have to part with her, but it was none the less a shock for me to realise the time had come. She was my constant companion and a great comfort and pleasure to me. I had taught her but could not give all the time she needed for her studies, and realised it was best for her to go to my mother and attend school regularly, and have the companionship of other girls. She was quite tall for her age, rode well, and was perfectly fearless, also hearty and strong, owing to the outdoor life in that wonderful climate. She was a great favourite with her little friends—the Thomas children, Orlando and Charlie Wilcox, and Max Weeks, with whom she played marbles, flew kites, and gathered wild-flowers.

One morning in the early spring we took her over to the town to join a lady friend who was going to San Francisco and would look after my child until she met her uncle. The Indians were quiet and on their reservations, and I felt it was the best time for her to go; she would be safe and I free from anxiety. The Colonel was under orders for an inspection trip, and I unable to travel, so we put her in the stage coach with four good horses that carried the mail. They went off in fine spirits, but when they got to Maricopa Wells, as there were no other passengers, they had to get out of the stage and go the rest of the distance on a buckboard. My child's dress was completely torn off her back from rubbing against a trunk, which she had to lean against for support. It must have been a terrible experience for them both. My brother said the little one looked like a young Indian when he met her at Los Angeles, she was so sunburned, covered with dust and dirt, and the waist of her dress torn in shreds. She interested the passengers greatly when crossing the Continent, telling them of her life in Arizona and her travels. Arizona was an unknown country then to the majority of people, as indeed it now is to many, and though most interesting to all who have sojourned there, none know what the development of this wonderful country will be.

When the Colonel was not on his inspecting tours we always had a little informal supper at 9.30. If game was in season we usually had it, for as I have said, he was an expert hunter and a fine shot, and when it was in season the rope stretched across the cellar was generally filled. We had long forks made especially to broil the birds, or to toast the bread with. After dinner the Colonel poked the fire so as to have plenty of hot coals by the time we needed them; then he mixed a toddy of some kind and got everything ready. The maid would bring in all the necessary things early in the evening and put them on the shelves for that purpose, for we had but few tables. We never had the servants wait on us at night. After the supper was eaten the Colonel, with the help of the youngsters, would carry the things back to the pantry; then the cigars would be lighted. What dear evenings they were! What thrilling reminiscences of the war the older ones would have to tell; what experiences in that Western country back in the fifties! I wish I could remember them accurately enough to tell them more in detail.

I think I have not mentioned that it was my custom

190

for several years to make beef tea and wine jelly twice a week for the hospital, after it was established, unless the doctor wanted it for a special patient. One day he stopped at the house and asked if I had either, and told me he would like me to have some for him every day for awhile, as a woman in the town was very ill and there was no one to make delicacies for her. For two weeks or longer he called every day, and I would tie up a bowl or small pitcher with a napkin, making a loop so that he could put his hand through to carry it. We people at the fort could get more delicacies through the commissary than the people in the town could procure, owing to the heavy express and freight charges. I remember my mother sent me out a fine gown and a hat, and the Colonel had a bill of twenty-four dollars expressage.

It was just about this time, when we were at dinner one Sunday evening, a man brought in a telegram. The Colonel took it, and while he was reading it turned very pale, and without speaking handed it to me. We had lost almost every dollar we possessed. The agent whom we were obliged to have, being so far from civilization, had speculated with our funds and our money was gone. I had then to learn economy. We talked the matter over fully. Schools had to be changed and one maid discharged. The Colonel from that day turned his pay over to me to do the best I could with it. It was very hard at first to make both ends meet, but I soon learned to economise, as every woman can when necessity demands it. While we were deploring the loss of our money our hearts were brightened by the birth of a daughter, Alice Wallace, named for my dear friend the wife of Captain Wallace of our regiment. Such a beautiful little treasure, to my mind, never was seen. There were three little ones born in the garrison that month, and when they were about a month old some officers came over from Fort Verde to visit us. When they came to our house, the Colonel carried the pretty blue bascinet into the parlour. There lay the cherub; she was a tiny thing, but like a Dresden China doll. The men said they would never again say all babies looked alike. When Alice was a few months old Mother Monica insisted upon our having our children baptised, as there was no clergyman at the fort, and although we were not Catholics the good father rode all the way from Tucson in a stage to Fort Whipple to baptise Nicholas and Alice. We had now been at Fort Whipple over five years. We knew every one for miles around the place, and the settlers were very fond of the Colonel; he got to know them well while hunting over the country. We also knew every one in the town without regard to caste; and whenever any delicacy was brought by the

stage a part of it was always sent to me. I remember
one day an officer,—Lieutenant Willcox,—came riding
rapidly up to our door, jumped off his horse, and ran
in saying, "Colonel, I have some fresh oysters, just
ten days from Baltimore." (The railway at that
time had gotten within three days of Prescott.) We
soon got a plate and the other necessary things. The
can was opened and there lay twelve fine fresh fat
oysters. Such a sight had never before been seen
there. They had been on ice all the way out. A man
coming into the Territory from Baltimore had
brought a half dozen cans which he had had specially
put up. They were delicious. The men stood by
seeing me enjoy them. I ate six, the lion's share,
and left them the rest. The Colonel afterward
learned that seven dollars had been paid for the
twelve oysters.

It was now time for us to have our auction. The
Colonel had been relieved from duty as Inspector
General, and was to join his regiment in another part
of the Territory. Notices were printed and sent
out nearly all over the county. I had selected a few
things we would need at Fort Grant, where we were
going for a short time; for as soon as the railroad
reached Willcox I was to go East and see my children once more. On the day of the auction the house
and grounds were crowded with people. I shut my-

self up in the nursery with the children and a few officers and ladies came to sit with me. After awhile I heard the auctioneer's loud voice asking for bids on a clock, and I wondered where it was. On opening the door a bit, I heard seven dollars bid. I hastily ran to the room and called out, "Don't bid on that clock; it don't keep time." It was the same clock that Dr. Davis had doctored—as he called it—years before. You can imagine the laughter from these hearty people, and Mr. Fisher, the auctioneer, said: "You must leave here; this is the only auction I don't want you to attend." There was a woman present who out-bid every one on the things in my sitting-room and bedroom. After the sale was over—and we realised three or four times more than we had expected—this woman sent a soldier to tell the Colonel she wanted to see him. She told him she wished me to use the things she had bought as long as I remained, and then she would come for them. The Colonel told her it was unnecessary, as I would stay with a friend until I left, but she insisted upon leaving them, nor would she give her address for the things to be sent to her.

Naturally the Colonel made inquiry about her, and found that the things had been bought for a poor frail woman in the town. It was she who had been so desperately ill a few months before, when the doctor

194

had gotten the wine jelly and other things every day for weeks. During her convalescence she had found a napkin on which my name was embroidered that had been wrapped around something sent to her, and she then knew who had been making the delicacies. The poor woman was much touched and deeply grateful, and said she wanted the things that I had used around her; surely the heart that held so much gratitude could not be wholly bad; here was compensation again.

A few days after the auction we were ready to again start on our journey across the desert, but to travel in a more southerly direction. We left Fort Whipple one beautiful morning, December fourth, Nick's birthday; he was just two years old. It was a funny sight to see our porch while the waggons were loading, the innumerable demijohns of spirits, wines, etc., etc., that were sent by friends for our journey (and to a man who rarely touched spirits), besides champagne-baskets filled with all kinds of good things to eat. The dear friends, many of whom we had known in joy, and sorrow, gathered round to say "Good-bye," and although I was anxious to get near the railway where I could the sooner reach the East and see my children, I left with one long tender regret, for the grave of my little son under the shadow of the great mountain had to remain. We

stopped for a few moments in the town as we passed
through, to say a last word to the friends who were
standing in front of the little post-office. Among
them were Mr. Curtis Bean, his wife and three most
beautiful children; Mr. Head, Mr. Richards, Mr.
Burmiester, and Mr. Spencer, a fine young man from
Vermont, who taught school. The officers at the garrison were very fortunate in being able to send their
children to him. I have learned that he has since
become a multi-millionnaire. It was an unusual sight
that day to see the crowd around our ambulance,—
gentlemen, miners, saloon-keepers, laborers, "Chris-
tians, Jews, Turks and infidels," one might say, yet
we liked them all and in the years spent among them
there had been no unkind word or deed and I shook
each one heartily by the hand and wished him good
luck.

Now we were really off. We climbed the great hill,
where I had first had a glimpse of the spot that was
to be my home, never dreaming so many years would
pass before I should be turning my back on it. The
Colonel had fixed the middle seat nicely for Alice
by lacing ropes back and forth quite high, so it was
impossible for her to fall off. I had put soft pillows
on the seat, and there the little lady sat during the
journey as happy as a bird. Nick often got out and
walked up the hills with his father and, although I

had no nurse, I got along finely. The children slept soundly and gave me no trouble whatever. We went over much the same ground for nearly two days that we had passed going into the Territory, but it was much more settled and at peace; no sign of Indians off their reservations; and we never dreamed there could be such trouble as old Geronimo caused later.

The third day we reached Phœnix, a nice, clean town, all green and white, with trees planted on all the streets. They had brought water in and it ran all around in "acequias" (small ditches) watering them. I am told that Phœnix is now a thriving city. Here we met Colonel and Mrs. Benjamin, going to Fort Whipple. He was to be the Adjutant General of the Department.

Starting on, we saw again in the distance old Montezuma's wonderful profile, that had affected me so much in the glimmering twilight as we went into the Territory. I am told that the Indians believe that one day he will rise and right things in the world, when the Pimas (Indians) and their friends will be found far ahead of the balance of mankind. As we went on we passed some wonderful specimens of cactus, some quite small and others from thirty to fifty feet high and from one to three feet in diameter. We also saw here in the valley of the Gila specimens of the "gigantic genus of cacti," which is, I am told, only found in this section of the world. The course of the Gila River is marked by a line of green, from which broad flats spread out on either hand, in some places fully fifty miles, with excellent soil. I am also told this has all been irrigated and enormous crops are now being raised there. Here on the Gila River the Pimas have their reservation. They are a peculiar people, different from other Indians, and have always been fast friends with the whites. They claim to have lived here forever and to be the original Aztec race, descended directly from Montezuma. There were about five thousand of them, but I suppose they are now fast disappearing. Many of them were used as scouts against the Apaches, with whom they had been at war for generations. On the Gila River are the remains of several cities presumably built by the Pueblos or Aztecs. The foundations and some of the walls are still standing.

We also passed through their villages, consisting of clusters of brush huts, cemented with mud, and lying at intervals along the road on both sides for the distance of six or seven miles. None but a few very young and very old men were in sight. Many squaws, who were very ugly, stood gazing at us from the doors of their domiciles, all of them naked to the waist.

Tucson is also in this southern part of the Territory. It is an exceedingly interesting old Spanish and American city, irregularly laid out and built in the usual style of adobe architecture. It is pleasantly situated in the Santa Cruz valley, but it was not very healthy at the time we passed by. There was also a fine military post, "Fort Lowell," and a delightful society, Spanish and American. It was in this southern part of the Territory that we saw the most remarkable mirages, great cities and castles, and churches with domes; it was almost impossible to believe they were not real.

Our journey was altogether delightful; no Indians, the weather perfect, the children and myself well, and plenty of game for the Colonel, to shoot. We enjoyed every moment, and I was sorry when we began our last day's march.

CHAPTER IX.

WE arrived at Fort Grant about three o'clock in the afternoon, and went at once to our own quarters, where we used our camping outfit until the waggons arrived with the furniture, etc. We took our meals for a while with Captain and Mrs. Thompson, who kindly took us in; they had been stationed with us at Fort Halleck, Nevada.

While we were there a strange thing happened. One morning, as we walked over to breakfast, the Colonel noticed the flag at half mast. He stepped on quickly and asked the sergeant of the guard what it meant. He replied that "in raising it, it had gotten caught and they had tried in vain to loosen it; so they thought they would leave it and perhaps the wind would blow it free." The Colonel said: "Come at once and take it down." They tried some time without effect, when the Colonel took hold of the rope and tried, remembering a trick he learned at sea many years ago. It was loosened and raised, and the Colonel told them never again to allow a flag to remain at half mast, when not for a death. While we were at breakfast that morning, some one knocked at the door, and Captain Thompson rose and went out to see a soldier. He had not returned many minutes, when he again left the table. I was sitting next to him and thought his expression strange, but said nothing for a while; however, as he did not return, I mentioned it to Mrs. Thompson, who said he always was interrupted at breakfast a number of times by soldiers. Still, I was not satisfied; I felt something was wrong, and finally she and the Colonel laughingly said: "Well, come along, and we will go hunt him up for you." His room was the back one on the other side of the house. Mrs. Thompson walked in and we heard a scream and, going to her, found Captain Thompson dead, lying across the bed on his face, where he had fallen and died, from apoplexy. I always regret I had not followed my instincts and insisted upon the Colonel going after him as soon as he left the table. Of course, we were all impressed with the fact that the flag had floated at half mast for thirty minutes. Was it a coincidence?

We had a nice double house, with courtyard in the center, in the Spanish style. It was built of adobe, with three rooms on each side opening out on a wide porch and garden; at the back of the garden were the stables. The soldiers came and helped me get the house in order. We took our breakfast at home, but went to the sutler's for luncheon and dinner. I had no nurse, but we had an excellent man who remained at the house while we went to dinner.

The day after the army waggons got in with the furniture, boxes, dogs, horses, etc., I missed Nick and started out to look for him, calling as I went, but got no response. I went on, and when within ten feet of the stable out rushed a setter dog that had been raised with Nick. They were just the same age, and had not seen each other since we left Fort Whipple, now over two weeks; he and Nick were playing together in the stable and the dog, hearing me call, must have thought I intended taking Nick from him again; for he rushed at me with his mouth drawn and kept me at bay. I was too much frightened to move and afraid to call the child, not knowing what the dog might do; however, in a few moments Nick came toward me, and the dog hung his head and tail and looked very sad. I took in the situation at once, and spoke kindly to "Tip," and we all walked on to the house. After that the Colonel arranged for the dog to sleep in the adjoining room to mine. I had no nurse and when we went to the sutler's for dinner, after the little ones were asleep, the Colonel would say: "Come, Tip, and take care of the children." He would lie down by their little beds and at a sound he would be up and bark. They needed no better caretaker.

202

I remember once at Fort Whipple I missed Nick, and opened the nursery door to look out for him. A funny sight met my eye. We used to make hash for the two dogs, Beauty and Tip. Each had his and her own tin pan that it was cooked in. What I saw then was Nick lying flat on his little stomach (he was not two years old), and he and Tip were eating out of the same pan. Another time I found them both together playing in the dog's house. They were devoted to each other. Tip was worthless in every other respect, but we always kept him and were fond of him on account of his great love for the children.

Fort Grant was beautifully situated at the foot of Mount Graham. The climate was perfect. I would spread a large comfortable on the floor of the porch for Alice to play on, and we would be out-of-doors all the day long. I would sew or read and watch the children. At six o'clock the little ones had their supper by the bright hearth fire and would go to bed. A fire during the day was unnecessary, even in winter. There were some agreeable people at Fort Grant, including Captain and Mrs. Overton and their young daughter, who has since written some interesting stories, where the scenes are laid in this vicinity; Lieutenant and Mrs. Geary, young, pleasant people; and Dr. Thomas and his dear old mother. I have often thought of her since, for her son died not long after I left the Territory.

One night we went to the sutler store for our dinner, where the bachelor officers had their mess. It looked like rain, which was very unusual, but the Colonel thought it would not come until midnight. While at dinner the rain came suddenly, and soon we heard a torrent roaring. On looking out, it was frightful. We waited some time, hoping it would hold up, but it did not; and the Colonel going out to see about getting some sort of a vehicle to take me home, found that the little dry creek that ran near to our house was a torrent, impossible to cross with any kind of carriage, or horse either. Two of our officers were drowned in just such a mountain torrent. A waterspout struck the head of the cañon and in a few minutes made a raging torrent of the little stream near which the troops were camped. "Both Lieutenants Henley and Rucker mounted their horses and assisted in carrying the rations (which were rapidly being carried away), to higher ground. On the last trip, coming out of the stream, Lieutenant Rucker made a safe landing, but Lieutenant Henley's horse was knocked down by the torrent and great rolling stones; the horse got out safely, but as Lieutenant Henley rose to the surface he was again knocked down, insensible. Lieutenant Rucker quickly uncoiled his lariat and riding close to the bank threw it across to his friend, who did not catch it; without thinking of the danger to himself, this fine fellow leaped his horse off the high bank ahead of Henley, and as the horse rose to the surface endeavoured to save him, but the torrent was fierce, and the gallant, noble-hearted fellow was swept from his horse, and he too was drowned.'' When this report reached the headquarters of the Department and was made known, there was universal sorrow throughout the whole Territory, where they were known and loved. That night we had to drive about four miles before we could get to the other side of the stream. It was the first of the spring rains and it washed the snow entirely from the mountain just back of us.

The life at Grant was very simple and very healthful. I never have breathed such invigorating air. The winter days were full of sunshine, and the atmosphere was so clear that I could stand on the porch and see the trains come in and go out at Willcox, twenty-three miles distant. I would watch often for the mail-rider and could see him when he seemed only a speck against the horizon. One not accustomed to watching would not know him for horse and rider, but soon we would see him on a hill, clearly outlined against the sky, miles away.

The railroad had been finished to Willcox, and I

was waiting for warmer weather in the East before starting on my trip to see the children. So many times I had planned to go, but something always happened to prevent; and now again it looked as though I would not get off, for I was suddenly taken ill with pneumonia.

And here I feel I must say a word about the medical corps of our army. These gentlemen are not only always ready to give willing service, but the very best that is in them, untiring and never thinking of self. Let the call come from the Colonel or his wife or the laundress or soldier's wife, each gets as devoted attention as the other. Not long ago I was in a garrison where the doctor was called in to attend the wife of a sergeant. He went and found it a serious case. After being there several hours and having his dinner sent to him, he sent to the hospital for a cot and rested a few minutes at a time, as he got the chance, and he never left the woman in the twenty hours, until she was safely delivered and she and the child doing well. An eminent physician of New York said to me one day that he could not understand men who were capable of passing the rigid examinations required by the Medical Army Board going into the service; that such ability would enable a man to reach the head of the profession in any city in a few years, whereas, in the army he received but a small compensation all his life for his services, without any chance to make anything extra, except by writing. This is all true.

As soon as I was able, I began to make my arrangements to go East, and Mrs. Hooker, whose husband had the most beautiful ranch in Arizona, "The Sierra Bonita," about six miles from Fort Grant, decided to go with me to visit her daughter, who was at school. We concluded not to take a nurse, but would take the drawing-room on the car and could keep the children there very well. Captain and Mrs. Overton kindly packed my trunks and boxes. I was not allowed to do anything, but to get strong and ready for the journey. The morning finally came for us to start, and it was with a beating heart I got into the ambulance to ride the twenty-three miles to Willcox, where we stayed all night. The Colonel put us on the train the next morning. Several officers had ridden over from Grant to see us off. Good-byes were said, "All aboard" called, and we were off.

There were but three passengers in our car besides Mrs. Hooker, the children and myself—a Roman Catholic priest and two Sisters of Charity, whom I was very glad to see. It seemed strange to me to be on a railroad train, especially in that part of the country.

The army has not been given the credit it deserves,

but the world is now fast awakening to the realisation that the Regular Army has been the great factor in building up, and for the progress in general of the great West. Soldiers made it possible for the great railways to be built across the Continent; they guarded the workmen from Indians, while they laid the rails, and afterwards, so that the rails should not be torn up, sleeping on the bare ground with only their blankets wrapped around them, often suffering from cold and exposure. The isolated army post made it practicable for the pioneer and early settler to take up ground, raise cattle and till the soil, for he, too, was protected by the soldier. Few people outside of the army realised the privations and suffering of the army officer and his family, for they bore everything uncomplainingly. Cut off from all intercourse of his kind, save the few in his garrison, perhaps a weekly mail of letters, and an occasional paper, for the distances for the mail-rider were too great for books and papers to be carried. The wives had generally the house-work to do, beside all of the sewing, and the care of the children, who were brought into the world without a nurse to look after the mother or child. Is it any wonder that many of these children died soon after their birth?

*　　*　　*　　*　　*

I know nothing of politics, but I know that a great

party in our country, running for election, proclaimed
that if elected they would cut down the army and
reduce the expenses of it. Was it ingratitude, or
ignorance of the fact that the army they would turn
down has made this great country what it is? Do
they not know that thousands of people in each and
every State hold the army dear to them? Too many
men, from the days of the Revolution, have given
up their lives, or have been wounded in the service
of their country, for their children, or grandchildren,
to forget it. My great-great-grandfather, William
Butler, was with Washington at Braddock's defeat.
My father gave willing and distinguished service to
his country for fifty years; my husband, brother, and
son are still serving. There are many, many families
in each State, like my own, and the halo will ever
remain over them. The party in this country that
will always win the goal will be the party that carries
on its banner, ''We will honor our Army for the
work they have done, in helping to make this great
country.'' I am but a woman, but I have helped
''bear the burden and heat of the day.'' Look back,
when the Colonel led that little band of officers and
men of the Sixth Cavalry down through that barbarous country where the foot of the white man had
never trod. Many of the men had their hands and
feet frozen, and the sufferings of all were terrible.

The fort was located, the officers and men remained, settlers came and made homes. It is now thickly settled and worth millions of dollars to the Government. Are such services as these men gave, to count for naught? It was also the army that constructed the telegraph lines and completed the great work of connecting the Pacific Ocean at San Diego with the Gulf of Mexico. A number of men were killed by Indians while doing this work, but the people knew nothing of it. I must say the Western railroads have shown their appreciation, for they cheerfully give the families of officers half-rate tickets over their roads, which enables many an officer to have his family with him.

The journey from Fort Grant was filled with anxiety. My little daughter was seriously ill from the change in the milk, and for hours after reaching New Mexico she lay in a state of collapse, from the high altitude. The dear Sisters of Charity were invaluable to me. We telegraphed ahead to have physicians meet us at the stations, which they did, and gradually the child got better. I don't know what I should have done had Mrs. Hooker not been with me; her sympathy, advice, and assistance, were invaluable, as she took entire charge of Nick, and as the baby got better I was able to get some rest.

When we got to a little town on the other side of the river from Kansas City we stopped for breakfast. It was blowing hard but we needed food and had to get out and go in a large, high, wooden building. We had just been served, when a man opened the door and called, "Run for your lives; this building will fall." Every one started, and two men passing near us each picked up a child and ran, Mrs. Hooper and I following as quickly as we could, but we were about the last to get out. We ran across the street and into a dug-out, where a cobbler was mending shoes. A tornado burst over the town, houses were blown down, trees were uprooted, and it was frightful. A heavy freight train was blown from the bridge into the river. All this time I had no idea where my children were, but, although I was anxious, I felt sure the men who had them would seek shelter. The storm in its fury lasted, I think, about thirty minutes, or more. The building we had been in was blown and scattered in every direction by the terrible wind. As soon as it was considered safe, Mrs. Hooker and I went out to try and find our train. The streets were so littered by the uprooted trees, roofs of buildings, and all kinds of débris that it was with difficulty we made our way. After being repeatedly directed we found the train and went aboard. It was hard for me to "possess my soul in patience" until I could again see the children. By and by I saw the men coming, carrying them as tenderly as possible. They told us the children had not been scared, and had been as happy as when they left us. Indeed, they were very enthusiastic about them and there was no lack of nurses to the end of our journey.

When we left Fort Grant the officers had put a basket of champagne in the drawing-room for us. I had forgotten it until now, and it seemed to me a good time to have some opened for everybody. I called the porter and told him to get some ice and to open some of the bottles, all of which was done. One man declined it, and, after we all had drunk some, he stood up and said that Kansas was a prohibition State and that there was a fine of fifty dollars apiece for any one drinking, and a double fine for the one who offered it. He scared us for a while, and then laughed and took some. He was right, however, about there being a fine for drinking. He knew it and thought he would have a little fun to cheer us up. Fortunately that energetic citizeness of Kansas that has made such havoc with her hatchet was not among the passengers.

The rest of our journey was comfortable, and we finally reached Philadelphia, where the two lads, Jack and Dave, met us and went on with us to my father's home. They had grown almost out of my recollection; they were great tall boys, the picture of health. I gazed at them in astonishment and could scarcely believe they were the little fellows I had left six years before, and that they really belonged to me. Somehow they had remained in my mind as I had seen them last, standing on the lawn of the school with hands clasped and with little sad faces. Now they were far bigger than I.

We arrived home safely. My parents and sisters were glad to see us again and also the dear little ones whom they had never seen. Alice looked up at my father with her great gray-blue eyes and held out her arms to him. He took her and held her close to his heart, and loved her devotedly from that moment; and anything she ever wanted he would have given her, if we had not been there to watch. I had taught both children that they must never touch anything on a table or bureau. I knew there would be so much more for them to see at home and I dreaded their handling things. When Alice saw anything that greatly pleased her she knew she must not touch it with her hands, so she would hold her little hands tight behind her and lean over and put her little lips or cheek against the desired object. My father had seen her do this several times, and it touched him, and he always insisted upon giving her what she wanted, but I would not yield. One day he left the luncheon table some time before we did, and when we went into the parlour my father had her on a large, soft rug in a corner of the room; he sat on a large chair in front, guarding her. He had given her all the little ornaments from the table to play with that she loved most. When we saw what she had and exclaimed our displeasure, my father rose and said, "he had some rights in the house which we did not seem to see," and that Alice should have some of the things to play with. It is easily seen I could not long maintain discipline.

In July of that summer I took a cottage at one of the well-known Virginia Springs, going for my own health as well as for the two younger children. The surrounding country was highly cultivated and the Blue Ridge Mountains, while beautiful, did not appeal to me as the great rugged peaks I had lived among so long (and indeed while memory lasts these great mysterious mountains will form a never-to-be-forgotten picture). The roads were good for riding and driving, which Nellie and the boys greatly enjoyed. It was an unspeakable pleasure to me to have all of my children—from whom I had been so long separated—with me, and the great stalwart boys could not be careful enough of me. There seemed a great peace in my heart.

The little ones had been unusually well. Alice had grown remarkably interesting for so young a child. Every day she was engaged by some of the ladies or the young girls, while Rosa, the nurse, got her meals. She was delighted with the gardens and her happiness was complete when she had a few flowers in her hand. One day late in August I saw she was not well and I sent hurriedly for a physician, who soon after his arrival sent for another, and I then knew my child's life was in danger. As soon as the children in the place heard of her illness they brought their little arms full of flowers for her, and they were put on her bed, where she could see them until the end; for in two hours from the time the doctor arrived the dear little heart that had given so much pleasure to every one who had ever come in contact with her had ceased to beat. There are some mortal sorrows. Her father always has a little blue sock in his bureau drawer which she wore in Arizona, and whenever he goes away from home it is tenderly laid in his trunk and goes with him.

I returned to Elizabeth, New Jersey, where, with the children, I remained until the winter of 1885. The boys then started out for themselves; Jack went on Mr. Hooper's ranch in Arizona, David had a position in New York, Nelly was at school at Ellicott City with Miss Sarah Randolph (the finest educator of her day), and I decided to take Nicholas and spend the winter in Washington, where I would be nearer Nelly and with my sister, Mrs. Harmony, whose husband, the Commodore, was on duty at the Navy Department. I enjoyed the winter greatly. The climate was mild and the city, with its broad streets and avenues flooded with sunshine, its gay parks and beautiful houses, to say nothing of the charming people one met from all parts of the world, was delightful to live in.

Later I had the great honor of being present at the reception given at the White House by President Cleveland and his wife. I shall never forget the scene as they came down the stairs and passed through the hall, lined on either side with diplomats from all countries in full court-dress, army and navy officers in full-dress uniform, judges of the Supreme Court, ladies in gorgeous gowns covered with jewels, Senators, Members of Congress, and civilians. As Mrs. Cleveland passed me on the arm of the President to go into the Blue Room I was thrilled with emotion; she was so young and fair and wore her honors so easily and gracefully that it was no wonder she won all hearts all over our land, regardless of party.

The Cabinet of President Cleveland was a very brilliant one. It was composed of men of fine intellect, who belonged to the old representative families of this country. Mr. Thomas F. Bayard was Secretary of State; his wife being very delicate, his beau-

tiful daughter Katharine—who afterwards died a very
sad death—and her sisters presided over their
father's house. Mr. Endicott—a Harvard man—was
the Secretary of War, and his wife and daughter
were most agreeable in their home. Mrs. Endicott
was an elegant, stately-looking woman with that
thoroughbred look which shows generations back of
one; Miss Endicott was also distinguished in appearance and had a very clever mind; she later married
Mr. Joseph Chamberlain, of England, who afterward
became Colonial Secretary.

Mr. William C. Whitney was Secretary of the
Navy, and represented the very best type of the
New York business man, and our navy made rapid
strides under his administration of the department.
His wife was the most charming hostess I had ever
seen; she had the rare faculty of making each one
feel he or she was the desired guest; many years
will pass before her gracious hospitality will be forgotten.

Another home which always had delightful after-
noons, was Mr. Donald M. Dickinson's, the Post-
master General. Mr. Manning was then the Secretary of the Treasury and it was always a pleasure
to spend a half hour there on their days at home;
indeed, as I have said, it was an unusual cabinet in
many respects. Mr. Lamar, the Colonel's friend,

was, as every one knows who ever met him, a most brilliant man; no one could know him well and not be fond of him.

There were other delightful hostesses among the residents of Washington. Mrs. Van Rensselaer Berry was quite the leader among the most exclusive set, and Mrs. McAllister Laughton was another, at whose house one always met delightful people from all over the world. Mrs. Loring, of Boston, had the nearest approach to a salon; there one always met men of distinction, judges of the Supreme Court, Senators, authors, and artists; the tone of her house was decidedly intellectual and enjoyable.

In 1886 the Colonel was ordered East, and we were temporarily stationed at Fort Myer, Virginia. Mr. Endicott, then Secretary of War, had said that the officers who had been on duty for so many years away from their regiments were to go back, and those who had been longest on the frontier were to come East, but I imagine he found it a difficult task to remove those who had been in Washington so long a time; they had taken root too deeply to be moved, as there were some who never served a day with their regiments. We, fortunately, for once in our lives, had a friend at court. The Secretary of the Interior, Mr. Lamar, went to the Secretary of War and called attention to the Colonel's record of

frontier service, and the Colonel was ordered to
report at the War Department, after having served
seventeen consecutive years in Arizona and New
Mexico; he had not seen his oldest boys for nine
years. We were ordered to Fort Myer, where we
had a large double house. It took some time to buy
the necessary furniture for it, for the Colonel was
so delighted when he got his orders East that he
packed his trunk, and left everything we owned there
for the officer who succeeded him; fortunately I had
brought the silver and a few treasures when I came
East. Fort Myer was not at that time a healthful
place; malaria prevailed and both the Colonel and
I had chills, but the drives back and forth from the
city were picturesque and beautiful and I enjoyed it,
besides there were large violet beds, some of them
under glass, and the roses were luxurious and beautiful. I remember picking a large basket full of
lovely pink bonsalines one morning late in November, and they were scarcely missed from the bush.
The view of the Potomac, the city and the capitol,
was fine, from our porch. Every morning and evening we watched the crows that flew over to the city,
regularly at eight o'clock, and returned at sundown,
great flocks of them. Our favourite walk was to
Arlington, only a short distance; it always made me
sad. I could not help regretting that a grave-yard

had been made of that home, which contained so many hallowed associations.

The following winter the Colonel was assigned to duty at the War Department, and we moved to Washington and took a house, where, for the first time in our married life, we lived in a large city. The few years that the Colonel had on duty in the East passed rapidly, for we had enjoyed every moment of it, having our children near us, and being surrounded with all that was delightful.

*   *   *   *   *

On April 1, 1890, he got orders to join his regiment. He was now Lieutenant-Colonel of the Fifth Cavalry. I did not go West with him, the doctor thinking it better for my health to remain East and I could not again leave my children, whom I felt needed me. Before the Colonel left it was decided that I should go to the mountains of West Virginia. My dear mother had died, my father was in feeble health, being in his eighty-sixth year, and I realised that the old home which had welcomed us all so heartily would soon be broken up. Ellen was now a young lady, and, having tasted to the full during the two years in Washington all that a society life could give her, had gone to Radcliffe College; and Nicholas, who had grown to be a strong, hearty lad, was at St. Paul's School. In 1893, when the Colonel

COLONEL (AFTERWARD BRIGADIER-GENERAL) JAMES BIDDLE, U.S.A.

came home on leave to be at our daughter's wedding, he had the pleasure of coming to his own home which I had built in his absence; and the out-door life in that healthful region, superintending the work of building our home, had completely restored my health.

We had a gay Virginia wedding on a most beautiful October day; the sun shone bright and warm, all doors and windows open, no place in the world being finer than the October weather at the historic old Berkeley Springs, the virtue of the water being well known to the Indians before the whites had possession. It was also the summer home of Washington, Charles Carroll, and Lord Fairfax, who presented the place to the State. It was through here that Washington and his men marched to Braddock's defeat. During the War of the States the two armies occupied it at different times, and the old court-house, with many of the records, was burned. Over fifty years ago it was the gayest place in the country, but that is all past. It is now the home of a few delightful people, who enjoy the water and the beauty of the surrounding country.

CHAPTER X.

THE COLONEL was now, and had been since 1891, in command of the Ninth Cavalry, and as Ellen was married, and Nicholas was soon to go to Harvard University, I went the following spring to join my husband at Fort Robinson, Nebraska. It was a large and very pretty garrison, with several rows of trees all around the four sides of the parade-ground, many of which the Colonel had put out, as he did in every frontier garrison of which he was in command. At Fort Lyon he planted several hundred, making four rows on all sides of the parade-ground. The water (the Arkansas River) was brought in from a higher point seven miles distant, Lieutenant Anderson being the engineer officer. The trees at Fort Robinson were not only a great beauty, but a great comfort, as the heat was intense during midsummer. They are now known as the Biddle trees.

Fort Robinson was remarkable for its society. In no city would you have found a more charming coterie then was there when I arrived. There were Major and Mrs. Chaffee; and, although the Major had not then acquired the great distinction which

QUARTERS AT FORT ROBINSON, NEBRASKA

CAPTAIN PHILIP PENDLETON POWELL, U.S.A.

has since fallen to him, his bravery and gallant conduct in many Indian encounters had won a name for him throughout the army; Lieutenant Philip Pendleton Powell, of Virginia, was the Colonel's adjutant, and his wife, who was a daughter of Judge Hicks of New York, was an unusually attractive woman.

Captain Stedman and his wife; Captain Garrard and his attractive, jolly wife; Captain Taylor, who was afterwards badly wounded in the Cuban War, and family; Captain Martin B. Hughes and his bright, clever wife (a Miss Stevens, of New York); also dear Jimmy Benton, who was quartermaster, and his young wife, who was the daughter of General Henry; and many others, married and single; but I must mention Lieutenant-Colonel Bernard, who looked like a great Norseman, he was so big and strong, with a long gray beard and head full of snowy white hair. The General was from the mountains of Tennessee and had enlisted during the Civil War, when the times were pretty hot down there. He was as brave as a lion, and had several medals and brevets, won in Indian fights. Major Isley and dear Dr. McEldery were also there.

The first change I noted in the garrison life from the early frontier days was the evening after my arrival. We were just finishing dinner, when two officers called and their cards were brought to me.

I was a bit surprised at the formality, as I had never seen a visiting card during all the years I had lived on the frontier; but I soon found that the life here was much more formal—they were not so dependent on each other. The fort was on the railroad. Books, magazines and papers were in profusion; and there was not only mental food, but a fine market was only twelve hours away, and we got everything good to eat through the canteen. Invitations to dinners were sent out a week in advance, and when seated at the table you would not have known you were not in Washington, or some large city, the silver, glass and china were so beautiful. The life was no longer simple (the greatest charm it had always had for me), but much the same as in a city; the only thing not changed was the old-time Friday Night Hop, always so enjoyable.

The country surrounding Fort Robinson was very curious. Great buttes (mountains of earth) rose up all around us, and in the distance looked like great castles. There was one great high butte about a mile from the fort that had an interesting tradition. It was said that many years ago the Sioux and Crows (Indians) were at war, and the Sioux finally succeeded in driving the Crows up this high butte toward nightfall; and, thinking there was no way for the Crows to escape, and not caring to fight at night, they rested at the foot until daylight, when they went up after them. All were gone, but the old men and old women. The Crows had killed their ponies and skinned them, and cutting the hides in strips, tied them together, and let themselves down this steep, perpendicular side one by one. The old men and women, who were not able to make a rapid escape, had been left to keep up the fires, so as to deceive the Sioux.

When I first went to Fort Robinson the bachelors invited me to join their mess, my husband being a member of it. One evening when we went to dinner I saw standing on the porch the largest Indian I had ever seen; he was at least six feet four inches tall, and his torso was tremendous. Dr. McEldery asked him, for me, if he had any Indian bead-work? He said he had and would bring me some the next day; he and his squaw were on a little vacation away from the Sioux Reservation on pass. He showed me a medal, which he wore around his neck, that President Tyler had presented to his grandfather for being a good Indian, and which was engraved on the medal. The next day I was in the sitting-room, reading, when I heard a gentle knock. Thinking it might be one of the little children in the garrison, who had brought me wild flowers several times, I got up quickly and opened the door. I was a bit surprised, for there stood the big Indian. He immediately

15   225

smiled and stepped in, saying, "Yes, yes, yes," and handed me a paper on which Dr. McEldery had drawn the row of houses putting mark X on the one we lived in. He seemed pleased that he had found it, and held up a bag. I asked if he had the moccasins? whereupon he turned the bag inside out, and there were several things. I asked, "How much?" and he slapped his legs, which I interpreted to mean a pair of trousers, and which was right. I went into the Colonel's dressing-room and got two pairs of old trousers that I knew were no longer wanted and returned with them; both pairs had suspenders attached, which seemed to give the Indian great pleasure. He had a large piece of cotton cloth wrapped round and round him, extending far below the waist, and I thought he had on a pair of old trousers. He had not had the clothes I gave him in his hands a moment when he gave the cloth wrapped round him a jerk, throwing the whole thing off; and there he stood naked, save for the clout he wore, and on each leg, tied just above the knee, were pieces of an old pair of trousers, which he also pulled off. I was considerably startled, but before running off to call the Colonel, who was in his room, I could not help remarking how very small his legs were, nothing but muscle and very thin, while his body was that of a giant.

At one time "Red Cloud," the famous chief of the

Sioux, came to Fort Robinson with a number of his
"braves" and some squaws to make a friendly visit,
having had permission from the "Great Father"
at Washington. As they walked into the garrison
in their full regalia, great war-bonnets with feathers
flying, the alarm and consternation of many of the
ladies may be imagined, although they had been told
the visit was expected. Few people, I imagine, can
see a tribe of Indians marching toward them, even
when not in their war paint, without feeling a
thumping of the heart and a trembling of the limbs;
at least that was my experience, but dear Mrs.
Bradner (Mrs. Powell's mother) seemed to have
plenty of nerve and shook hands immediately with
Red Cloud on his arrival. They remained several
days at the fort and gave a war dance which was
attended by people living many miles distant.

The life here was very pleasant; the quarters were
excellent, and with good plumbing, the first I had
seen in the army. The houses stood back, with green
plots in front and at the sides. There were about
a dozen sets of quarters (two houses under one roof),
and they all faced the parade-ground, which was
very large, fully six hundred feet square, while off
to the right of the garrison was a magnificent drill
ground. The water was brought in from a distance
of several miles, and ran in acequias (little ditches)

all around the place to water the trees; it was hard to make the grass grow, but no effort was spared and the place was beautifully kept.

In June, 1895, Lieutenant-General Schofield came to Fort Robinson to inspect the regiment. He was making the final inspection tour of the army before his retirement. I think I cannot do better than give the General's report:

FORT ROBINSON, NEBRASKA.

COLONEL JAMES BIDDLE, NINTH CAVALRY,

Commanding Fort Robinson.

I am directed by the Lieutenant-General commanding the Army to convey to you his sense of pride and satisfaction in his recent inspection of Fort Robinson at finding the troops under your command in all respects in a high state of efficiency, and prepared for active field service. Besides which, it was highly gratifying to find your regiment so thoroughly instructed in all the duties prescribed by the regulations for occasions of ceremony, and all of the complicated maneuvers attending the inspection and review of the troops, both in full dress uniform and in campaign dress and equipment and in battle exercises. Every portion of all those exercises was performed with great accuracy.

As an old companion in arms, who well recollects your meritorious services during the period of the Civil War, the Lieutenant-General is especially gratified to be able to pay you this high and justly deserved compliment. Very respectfully

Your obedient servant,

(Signed) J. P. SAWYER,

Lieutenant-Colonel, Mil. Secty.

It was only natural that the regiment, officers and men, were greatly pleased with this report. They knew how hard the Colonel had worked to bring about the result; day after day he had drilled them himself, and indeed he did so until the day he retired; and I think I can safely say that no regiment was ever turned over to a successor in finer condition.

During the summer of 1895 two charming girls came to visit us—Miss Chismore and Miss Edith Pendleton. They had a very gay visit, as all girls do in a military post—riding, driving, dancing, dinners, and all the pleasures incident to a visit in a garrison. We also went to Fort Niobrara, by invitation of the officers and their wives, and had a most delightful visit; the girls were given all kinds of entertainments, beginning with a very enjoyable musical, given by Captain and Mrs. Hascall, and ending with a play, given by the officers and ladies of the post the night we left. Our train was due at Valentine that night at one o'clock; when we came out of the hop-room to get in the ambulance to drive to the station, six or seven miles distant, we found it was pouring rain and the wind howling over the desert. They begged us to remain, but we were due at Hot Springs, South Dakota, the next night. Lieutenant Elliott and Lieutenant Drew were to accompany us there; it is sad to relate that both of these promising young officers succumbed to the Spanish War. Lieutenant Elliott was a specially brilliant young man, having a fine intellect. The troops at Fort Robinson had been going for several years to the Hot Springs on their yearly practice march, and every one in that part of the country was fond of the Ninth Cavalry; they were so well drilled that people came from far and near to see them, and their fame was well known in the West and at the War Department long before the Spanish War. Mr. Evans, the proprietor of the fine large hotel, had invited all of the officers and their families, as well as those of the Eighth Cavalry, to a ball given in honour of the Ninth. It was done in true Western hospitality; one wing of the hotel was set apart for the use of the officers and their families, and we were to be Mr. Evans' guests for forty-eight hours. The ball-room was beautifully dressed with flags and candles ready for lighting, and the bands of both regiments were to be present. Among the officers from Fort Meade were Colonel Carleton, wife and daughter, Captain John Johnson and his delightful wife and daughter. (Captain Johnson afterwards resigned, much to the loss of the service, but not before he was promoted to the rank of brigadier general for distinguished service.) There were also Lieutenant Duff and wife, and many others.

At one time it looked as though we would not get
there. The storm became intense and the mules
would not face it; the night was frightfully dark
and the road dangerous in many places; the wind
blew a hurricane, it rained in torrents, and we were
all dripping wet; Lieutenant Drew spoke to the
driver to try and get him to urge his mules on, but
the driver said they would not face the storm and,
indeed, it became frightful; but by and by I
began to suspect the driver a little, and put my
head out of the door and said, "My man, we have
got to reach that station some time to-night, as we
are not going back, and if you will get us there
in time to catch the one o'clock train I will give
you five dollars." There was no further trouble
and we heard no more about the mules stampeding.
The man had wanted the young lieutenants to "put
up" something, but they did not recognise the "old
soldier" game as quickly as I did; and we made our
train. Fortunately, we ladies had a private car, as
there was not a dry piece of clothing on any of us.

We reached Hot Springs, Dakota, the next morning, no colds and no discomfort resulting from our
disagreeable ride over the desert. We met all the
officers and ladies of the Ninth, as well as many of
the Eighth Cavalry, among them were Colonel Carl-
ton and wife, Lieutenant Johnston with his charm-

231

ing wife and little daughter, Lieutenant Duff, and many other delightful people, at the hotel. After unpacking our trunks, we went together to have a swim in the magnificent pool about a quarter of a mile distant from the hotel. It was a gay party that walked up the springs that lovely September morning. Miss Chismore and Miss Pendleton, being excellent swimmers, went to the deepest part of the pool with several others, where there was a good bit of fun and frolic. The pool there is much the finest I have ever seen, and the water is so graduated that children can play in it and learn to swim without danger.

We had not been in the water long, when Mrs. Benton asked if any one had seen her husband, who shortly before had been sliding down the toboggan and doing all kinds of tricks in the water. The officers told her they thought he had gone out of the water, as indeed we all thought, (he was a fine swimmer and an all-round athlete), but Mrs. Benton became anxious, and indeed almost frantic, declaring that she knew he was drowned; and she went out of the pool to dress and look for him. After she had gone the good swimmers were having a race, when suddenly a terrible thing happened. Lieutenant Preston touched something at the bottom of the pool, which proved to be Lieutenant Benton.

232

He was dead. He had died of heart disease. There was not a drop of water in his lungs. The shock was terrible to us all, for every one loved him. It can hardly be imagined what it was to his devoted young wife; but I never saw a braver woman. She was a worthy daughter of General Guy V. Henry. We all went quietly back to the hotel, packed our trunks, and took the afternoon train for Fort Robinson. The ball, of course, did not come off.

I shall never forget his funeral, which was a few evenings later; it was quite the saddest and most affecting I ever saw. The train for the East left at 9 P.M. The command all turned out. The band played Chopin's Funeral March (which he loved) from the time we left the house until the train bearing his body left. The escort and the gun-carriage, bearing the coffin draped in the flag, went first, followed by his horse; then there were several carriages; the troops following with arms reversed, and many men carrying lanterns, as the night was intensely dark. It was very solemn and impressive, and made a picture I shall always remember. The Colonel went to Chicago with Mrs. Benton, where some of her family met her.

The garrison did not recover from the shock for some time. Miss Chismore and Miss Pendleton had sent invitations out to all the military posts in the

Department for a ball they intended giving in return for the many courtesies they had received, but the invitations were recalled.

In the early autumn of the year 1896 Captain Anderson, who was in command of the Yellowstone Park, invited me to bring the young ladies who were visiting me to the Park. The girls were greatly excited over the prospect of seeing this wonderful place, and we hurriedly got ready—as it was late in the season—and left Fort Robinson one beautiful September morning on the Burlington Road, seeing the Custer battle-field and many Crows and other Indians *en route*.

We missed our connection at Billings and had to remain several hours, but the place was full of interest, and I saw more really fine Indian curios than ever before. The Indians, dressed in their gay blankets, walked about quite unconcerned and no one paid any attention to them. After a very pleasant day we took the train for Cinabar, where Captain Anderson met us. We found General Miles on the train, having a special car, Mrs. Miles, Senator Sherman, Mr. and Mrs. Wiborg of Cincinnati, Dr. Hoff, U.S.A., Colonel Michler, and some other officers of the General's staff were with him. They went to the Mammoth Springs Hotel, where we had the pleasure of spending the evening with them.

CAPTAIN GEORGE S. ANDERSON, U.S.A.

Early the next morning they started out for a tour of the Park, while we explored the wonderful Hot Springs, and I saw many old friends among the officers and their families stationed there. The next morning, greatly to our delight, who should arrive but General Coppinger with a party of gentlemen, going south of the park on a hunting trip. They were admirably equipped. They had just come from Fort Robinson, where they had been fitted out with men, horses, mules, and indeed everything the Colonel could give them. It cost the Government nothing and was good experience for the men, who profited greatly by the trip. They told us the Colonel had given them a regimental drill and review, which they declared the finest thing, in a military way, they had ever seen, and they were most enthusiastic over the Ninth Cavalry.

These gentlemen were travelling like princes. They had a private train with ten cars for themselves, with compartments, and most of the compartments had bath-rooms; they also had box-cars for their horses. Dr. Webb had brought letters to the Colonel, and they were all most anxious to see the regiment drill, as they had heard so much of it. The Colonel not only gave the drill, but the eight troops turned out in full uniform and were reviewed; then they put on field dress and were again reviewed, fully

235

armed and equipped for the field—saddles packed,
two field-guns on pack-mules, twenty-six mule teams
with baggage-waggons, two ambulances with hospital
field supplies, surgeons and men, complete; a signal-
man was with each squadron and one with the commanding officer. After the review the waggons were
packed, and the squadrons went through all the prin-
cipal drill movements required in battle, advancing
and firing both mounted and dismounted as skir-
mishers, and by troop; also in extended order; the
field-guns were taken off the pack-mules, mounted and
advanced firing, shelling the hills. I could well understand their enthusiasm, for, notwithstanding the
hundreds of times I have seen it, I am yet, always
thrilled with excitement.

The morning after the hunting party left, we
started off for a tour of the Park. We left the Mammoth Hot Springs at about eight o'clock in the morning. A light snow was falling, but we were well
equipped for all kinds of weather and did not mind
it. We stopped for luncheon at Norris' Geyser
Basin, a most wonderful place, with its spouting
geysers, clouds of vapour and overpowering odours of
sulphur. From there we went to the Fountain Hotel,
where we stayed two days, there being so much to
see, both at the upper and middle basins. The drives
were delightful, as the roads were perfect. We saw

quantities of game, and were told that too much credit could not be given Captain Anderson for his protection of game in the Park. At every turn something wonderful was to be seen, impossible to describe. We had a lovely sail on the beautiful Yellowstone Lake, which is 7788 feet above the sea and is, I am told, the largest lake at a great elevation in North America, its dimensions being twenty miles north and south and fifteen miles across. Perhaps the most wonderful things we saw were the petrified trees or fossil forests; the annual rings show some of the larger trees to be at least five hundred years old.

It is impossible for me to relate all the wonders we saw, but I must say a word about the Grand Cañon, which I would like every one in our country to see. We got out of the ambulance and walked up a trail until we came to a jutting rock, which the Captain had enclosed with a strong railing, which was necessary, for one's head is apt to get dizzy as you step out on this rock. The grandeur and beauty of the place is overpowering, and I burst into tears. On either side are vast pinnacles of sculptured rock, and the water passes with a single bound hundreds of feet into the gorge below. The colours of these rocks are wonderful; they look as though rainbows had settled on them—the moss green, browns, yellows of all shades, crimsons, and purples; an artist with his brush could not tell it. We watched it for hours, going and returning many times during the day, and again by moonlight in the late evening. Surely there can be nothing more beautiful. I have since visited the Grand Cañon of the Colorado, which must be the most wonderful thing in nature—certainly, the most awe inspiring. It is vastly larger and grander in every way, but to my mind not nearly so beautiful. The next day we returned to Norris' Basin. This basin is considered the oldest in the Park, and there is much that is both wonderful and attractive, and I think we enjoyed seeing the spouting geysers, the clouds of vapour, the great mud pots, the Emerald Pool, and the "Great Monarch" (who spouted in regal splendour for us), more even on our return than we had on starting out. Here we remained one night, seeing everything leisurely. Next morning we started for the Mammoth Hot Springs, where we remained one day, going again over the wonderful formations, impossible to describe. We then turned our faces toward Fort Robinson. The girls were both dear lovers of nature and had thoroughly enjoyed every moment, and the Captain assured me, when I was thanking him for the pleasure he had given us, that he was amply repaid by their appreciation and great enjoyment. A few weeks after our return, General Coppinger (who was in command of the Department), and the party of gentlemen, returned from their hunt. The party consisted of Dr. Seward Webb, Mr. Louis Webb, Captain Robert Emmet, formerly of the Ninth Cavalry; Mr. Jack Purdy, a very delightful man, and several others. The Colonel gave them another review. It was really very thrilling to see the charge these soldiers would make across the great drill-grounds. The girls and myself generally went out to see them every day, and we did not wonder that these civilians enjoyed it as much as they did. After the review they returned with us to luncheon. Just as the salad was being served the funeral call sounded and the Colonel excused himself, saying one of his men was to be buried, and he made it a rule to attend the funeral of any soldier who died in his command. General Coppinger went with him. After they left I saw a very serious look come over the face of Captain Emmet, and he asked me if he might also be excused, as the man to be buried was in the troop he had commanded in the Ninth Cavalry before he resigned. I well remember the first time I saw this gallant young officer. It was at Fort Grant, Arizona, about 1881, or thereabouts. One terribly cold, stormy night the Colonel and I were sitting close by the bright hearth-fire when we heard a knock at our outside door. As I was nearest the door and the Colonel was reading, I quickly jumped up and went to the hall to open the door, followed closely by the Colonel, for a knock at the outer door was unusual, and both of us had been a little startled. The officers of the garrison usually came into the hall, and then knocked. When I opened the door there stood a man in soldier's uniform—the long blue overcoat, with belt filled with ammunition, a soft gray felt hat, or sombrero, and high top boots, with trousers tucked in. I knew at a glance that he was an officer, and as he stood against the outer darkness, with his hand resting on his gun, he formed a picture in my mind never to be forgotten. As I have said, the night was black and stormy, and he had marched from Fort Apache with fifty Indian scouts, and he was the only officer with them. He had slept on the ground, rolled in his blanket, during the whole long march over mountain and desert. He had just arrived, and called on the commanding officer to report. These Indian scouts, who were considered peaceful, were the very creatures who shortly afterwards killed Captain Hentig. They used to come prowling around our house trying to see my little children, Nicholas and Alice, whom they thought very beautiful, on account of the light hair and blue eyes. I think I mentioned going into the kitchen one day and finding eight or ten Indians sitting in a circle on the floor; they had the two children in the ring, all playing with them, and strange to say the little ones were not the least afraid of the Indians, and did not wish to go in the house with the nurse.

But to return to our luncheon. After Captain Emmet left, I asked the other gentlemen if they would like to go and see the funeral, and it pleased me greatly that they all left their luncheon and fell in line after the men and marched to the soldier's grave. It is needless to say the whole command appreciated this act of respect shown to the dead soldier. About five o'clock (P.M.) the Colonel, Captain Powell, Lieutenant Eugene Ladd, who had accompanied the hunting party in charge of the men, Miss Pendleton, Miss Chismore and myself went down to the special train, and saw the car-load of elk, deer, and other game; it told the story of the glorious time the hunters had had.

CHAPTER XI.

A few months after this—December 11—came the day for the Colonel's retirement from active service. The evening before, at a little dance given us, the Colonel was presented with a very beautiful loving cup by the officers of the regiment. It was very unexpected, and the Colonel was much touched and made a charming little speech, which surprised me greatly, for he was always a man of but few words; but the occasion inspired him.

The day we left Fort Robinson was one of the saddest I remember. The men were devoted to the Colonel, and all during the day they came one by one to shake his hand and to say ''Good-bye,'' tears rolling down their cheeks. In the late afternoon Professor Gungl brought the band to the house for a last serenade. They played all the Colonel's favourite pieces. He was very fond of music and had always taken great interest in the band. Professor Gungl was a fine musician and had brought the band to a fine state of efficiency. Every morning they played at the Colonel's office, and on Sunday evenings, when we were always at home informally, Mr. Gungl would bring his violin, of which he was master. Miss Chismore was a fine pianist, while Mrs. Gardner and one or two others sang delightfully.

The night we left "Fort Robinson" the whole command, including the band, also all of the ladies, went to the station to see us off. The train came along about nine o'clock, and the passengers wondered what was happening. As we pulled out of the station we heard the cry of the men; it was like the wail of the wind through a pine forest; I can never forget it. The Colonel was greatly affected and sat in silence. His long service was over. He had started out at the first call in 1861, joining the Tenth New York, of which he became quartermaster; he was shortly transferred as Captain to the Fifteenth U. S. Infantry, and was soon after ordered to Indiana to pay the soldiers of that state the "advance bounty." He then went to Richmond, Kentucky, to pay the Seventy-first Indiana Volunteers, that had been hurried off to the front to meet "Kirby Smith." On arriving there he found the regiment encamped about a mile from town. He showed them how to make their camp and fix their tents in proper manner, thus becoming identified with them. He had just finished paying them, when the pickets were fired upon. The Lieutenant Colonel asked him to take command of the regiment, but he could not as he and the Major ranked him; however, he went into action with them, and after the Lieutenant Colonel and Major were killed, he commanded the regiment until the battle was over. After the regiment's return to Indiana for reorganisation, the officers and men petitioned the Governor to appoint him their Colonel, and Governor Morton, the great War Governor, gave the regiment to him. It was afterwards known as the Sixth Indiana Cavalry, and served until the close of the war.

The Colonel was also in command of a brigade in General Stoneman's Cavalry when he was captured at Macon, Georgia. He also commanded a brigade under General Johnson, serving until the close of the war, receiving several brevets, one of Brigadier General for "long, gallant, and meritorious services during the war." After the war was over, he again joined his regular regiment, the Fifteenth Infantry, from which he was soon transferred to the Eleventh Infantry, and after the reconstruction of the States he was transferred to the Cavalry; he then went to the frontier, having, with the exception of three years, almost continuous Indian service, and yet he, with many others having fine records, was retired as a Colonel, clearly showing that an officer's record does not count for much without political backing, and I fear the army (unlike the navy) will be always more or less influenced by politics, for the reason that many

Senators and Members of Congress think that in case
of war they could take command of a brigade or
division, as several have done and left gallant records,
while they all recognise they could not command a
battle-ship, either in peace or war.

The story of the Colonel's capture and exchange
has interested so many of his old and new friends that
I think I will give it, in his own words, as he told me
the story after his return. Although he fared so much
better than many others he lost over sixty pounds
during his imprisonment, and my dear mother did
not recognise him when she saw him, until he told
who he was.

He was taken prisoner about twenty miles from
Macon, Georgia, but, as I have said, I will give it in
his own words:

"I was in command of Biddle's Brigade in General
Stoneman's Cavalry, that held the left of the line
of General Sherman's army at the investment of
Atlanta. One morning of August, orders came from
General Stoneman for me to pick out of my brigade
all the horses that were capable of making a very
long run. I was able to get about two hundred men
sufficiently well mounted to comply with his orders,
and was ready to move out from the left next morning with 120 rounds of ammunition per man, and the
main portion of a ration (not including meat) to last

ten days. In the morning I was in line at the designated spot awaiting further orders. General Stoneman soon arrived and we moved out with about 1400 men and a battery of light artillery and took up the march, passed round the right flank of Hood's army, down the railroad, to wait at Macon. We moved night and day with very short intermissions for rest, two hours being the longest I remember. We had flankers out on each side of the road with orders to bring in any suspicious parties, light waggons and bacon whenever it could be obtained. As I have said, we moved with great rapidity, stopping only to feed the horses when we came across any grain, and also to replenish the nose bag or tie a bundle of unthrashed grain on the horses. As we neared Macon, we had a few slight skirmishes with the Confederates, who were evidently out seeking information. There had been a small squadron of the Third Indiana Cavalry sent eastward to destroy a railroad bridge. It accomplished its work and rejoined us. Some time after, on approaching Macon, we drove in the Confederate outposts, but when we reached the ford we found it impossible to cross, the river was so swollen, and citizens informed us they had never known it to be so high at that season of the year. What planking there had been on the railroad bridge had been removed, and besides, a battery in a small earthwork on the Macon

246

side commanded the bridge. After the situation had been closely observed, there was nothing left for General Stoneman to do but to turn back and face the large body of pursuers that we felt sure had followed us from Hood's army. After going about ten miles we struck their advance guard and drove them back until we came on the main body, commanded by General Iverson. We battled with him for most of the day until our flanks were turned and driven in, when General Stoneman told me to hold the ground as long as I could with the few men I had left and he would send me word later what to do. Lieutenant Colonel Matson, commanding the Sixth Indiana Cavalry (my own regiment), sent me word that his ammunition was about exhausted. I sent word for him to divide his ammunition among his men and to fall back and remain at some little distance until he heard further from me. General Stoneman and his staff were with me, besides the few men I had of the Fifth Indiana Cavalry, when we found we were surrounded (the other brigades having left). The Sixth Indiana Cavalry, finding the Confederates had lapped between us, had also gone, and there was nothing for General Stoneman to do but surrender with the few men and myself that were left. I found the officer in command of the Confederates was Colonel Cruse, of Georgia, a gallant officer, whose command I had often had skir-

mishes with, and with whom I had become acquainted.
He took me in charge and I stayed with him that night,
and he asked Colonel Iverson to allow me to ride into
Macon with him, the following morning, where I was
to be put into the officers' prison. I here refer to an
occurrence that took place that was the cause of my
being able to do some acts of kindness to my prison
companions and was the ultimate means of my being
exchanged.

"Shortly before I was captured my adjutant, Lieutenant G. A. Brown, came to me and informed me that
he had captured a Confederate tax collector with con-
siderable money, and asked what he should do with it.
I told him to bring the money to me and let the man
go. Shortly after he came, bringing a roll of Confederate bills, which I put into my saddle-bags. On
arriving at the prison I dismounted and put my
saddle-bags over my arm to go in. As I walked in I
saw on the other side of the fence a lot of officers of
Stoneman's command. No one seemed to pay much
attention to me, as I was put in alone, and I asked one
of the officers what they were doing there. He said,
'We have been searched to see what money or papers
we might have.' I said, 'Have you been searched?'
and on his replying in the affirmative, I took my
saddle-bags quietly off and threw them to him, telling
him to keep them for me. Shortly after I was called

up and searched and the few dollars I had in green-backs and some official papers were taken from me, and I was sent into the prison. I soon found my friend with the saddle-bags and found the healthy wad of Confederate money secure. After going into the prison we were assigned to our bunks; there were two or three tiers under a roof supported by posts but with no side walls. There was a walk outside of the posts and outside of the walk was a low fence, then a space of about twenty feet between the low fence and a high fence, where there was a walk on which the sentinel marched up and down on his post. To step over the low fence, which was called 'the dead line,' subjected you to being shot. During the time I was in the Macon prison, General Stoneman, his staff and I messed together. The officers of my own regiment did not come to the prison until some time later, as they were not captured until they had gone a con-siderable distance from where General Stoneman sur-rendered. I kept the mess well supplied out of the Confederate funds and we lived well. But the com-manding officer got some inkling that the officers had considerable money and were spending it at the post-trader's, but the latter was kind enough to have his boy inform me there was to be a search made, so I took the money, rolled it in small rolls, stood up in my bunk and shoved it between the rafters and shingles before the officer came to make the search. Of course nothing was found, and the search was made a second time with the same result, as I had again been informed.

"After we had been in the Macon prison about six weeks we were moved to Charleston, South Carolina, and were put in the building known as 'The Castle,' down by the water front. General Stoneman, his staff and myself were put on the lower floor of the tower under fire of our guns from the earthworks and fortifications. The shells came screeching over and landed in the upper part of the town, passing right over our heads. Previous to our arrival some of the shells had burst over the tower; the holes were plainly seen that were made by the pieces of the shells in the ceiling of the room to which we were assigned. With the exception of the General, we all took turns in cooking and caring for the room. I continued to keep the mess in pretty good shape, with the balance of the money I had brought with me. One day the General said, 'Biddle, I don't know what I would have done without you.' I replied, 'I am glad that I have been able to help, but I think you ought to appoint me Chief Commissary.' 'Why, yes,' he said, 'I'll do it.' I little thought when he joked how important it would be to me afterward. While we were in the Charleston Castle a report came that General Morgan and his brother had been captured in the North and there was some talk of having them hung. The report was, that if this were done Stoneman and I were to be treated in the same way, but there was nothing in it.

"One day when it was my turn to be cook and room orderly I had tidied things up; the others had gone out in the yard to sun themselves, and I was alone watching the beans cooking in the soup, when a Confederate officer came into the room and asked if I were General Stoneman. I replied, 'No, but General Stoneman will be in shortly.' He then said, 'Here is a paper which I will leave for General Stoneman and his officers, and I will return soon.' He went out, leaving the roll of paper lying loose on the table. I reached over, took the paper and read it. It was a parole of honor for General Stoneman and staff to make no attempt to escape while travelling to an exchange station to the north of Macon, near Atlanta. It was a pretty sad paper for me to read, to see that these gentlemen were going home fine and fat from my care and I to be left. I sat by the fire thinking deeply when a thought flashed through me. I pressed my finger to the side of my nose, and looking up said, 'Oh! Ho!' and felt quite comfortable. Shortly General Stoneman and Colonel Keough came in. Stoneman picked up the paper, read it and passed it to

Keough and then to the other officers, who all looked over at me sorrowfully, knowing I knew the contents. The Confederate officer soon returned, when I presented him to the General. He then asked the General if he and his officers were willing to agree to it. The General assented and sat down to the table and signed it. As he arose Keough started to sit down, but I motioned him back, seated myself in the chair and wrote: 'James Biddle, Sixth Indiana Cavalry, Chief Commissary.' A look of astonishment passed over their faces. After all had signed and the officer gone, Stoneman looked at me and said. 'How could you do it? You are a brigade commander.' I replied, 'General, I am no brigade commander, I am a prisoner of war; and do you remember a little conversation we had a few days ago about my providing for you all so comfortably and you appointed me chief commissary of the staff?' He said, ' You are right, and I hope it will get you out,' and they all seemed glad that I might have a chance.

"The next morning we packed together our few little things and started for the front. The report of my getting out had evidently gotten around, for the imprisoned officers lined the way and I had many congratulations and good wishes for my success, and away we went by rail to the front, about thirty miles from Atlanta. When we reached there I found General

252

Iverson and Colonel Cruse. Iverson said, 'Why, Biddle, you are a brigade commander and not a chief commissary.' So I told him how it all occurred, and said, 'Colonel, we are both cavalrymen and have been hammering at each other for a long time; can't you help me out?' They had a little talk together and then explained that there had not been enough men sent in to exchange me, 'but,' General Iverson said, 'we will parole you and give you a pass to go to headquarters and see if General Sherman can give you enough men to exchange you; we are not to meet until day after to-morrow. It is about twenty miles to where the transfer is to be made. If there are not enough men to exchange for you, you will give no information whatever but will return here and give yourself up.' I accepted gladly and got off early in the morning, after having eaten a good breakfast. General Iverson gave me a pass to protect me from any Confederates I might meet and General Stoneman gave me a hard boiled egg, which he had sat on the day before, and that was all I had to eat on that twenty-mile walk. I ran on one patrol of cavalry, showed my pass and told what I was trying to do; they treated me kindly, wished me luck and bade me 'Good-bye.' The only other persons I saw were a man and his wife coming to get some rations and they had nothing to eat with them. I walked on and was not as weary as I expected, having a hopeful heart and a mashed egg.

"Toward evening I happened to look along the road and saw sitting on his horse, at the top of a slight ascent, with his carbine at an advance, a man in blue—a picket of our army and one of the eyes of the army. I slipped into the brush, overcome with emotion, and waited for my heart to cease beating as it did before I stepped out for him to challenge me, for I don't know what I could have replied. At last I moved out into the road and he saw me. A voice called, 'Halt! who comes there?' I answered, 'A friend.' He called, 'Corporal of the Guard, Post No. 1,' and shortly after the corporal rode up and questioned me. I showed the pass and told who I was. (I had on a pair of corduroy riding trousers, blue flannel shirt, and top riding boots, and a slouched gray hat I had bought at Macon. I was covered with dust and did not look much like the party I represented myself to be.) He took me to the picket-post, where there were a few mounted soldiers, and told me they were soon to be relieved and they would take me to General Belknap's headquarters. General Belknap commanded the troops covering that portion of the front. I sat down with the men to rest, and asked the corporal if he had anything to eat. He said they had eaten everything up. I then asked if the men would scrape out the bottoms of their saddle-bags and see if there were not a few crumbs of hard tack. They soon raked up nearly a cup full and three little pieces of bacon—one with the marks of the teeth of the last biter. I borrowed a spoon, went down to the creek, soaked the crumbs and ate my supper.

"The relief came soon and we went to headquarters. The corporal went to General Belknap and reported the circumstances of the meeting and bringing me in. The General immediately sent for me but I saw that he was rather suspicious. After talking a while he asked me if I would have a drink. I accepted with pleasure, as I really needed it, and took a big one. He said to me years after, when talking the matter over, 'Biddle, I was very suspicious of you until I saw you take that drink.' After a good supper he sent me in an ambulance to General Sherman's headquarters in Atlanta, where I arrived quite late in the evening. I reported to the Adjutant General, telling who I was, and was then taken to the General, to whom I told the whole story. After hearing it he said, 'Biddle, I am awfully sorry; I have exchanged every man prisoner I have.' I then said, 'General, I have to go immediately back.' The General told me the exchange party would go down by train to meet the Confederate officers with General Stoneman and staff and I could go with them. I asked the General where

I would find the Paymaster, who gave me a month's pay, as I had given away all the Confederate money when I left.

"The next morning I was at the train when the three officers who were to go to the exchange came down. The clerk with them had a bundle of rolls and one of the officers a round bundle under his arm. We got into a box-car and were off. Going about half the distance I had walked we met the other train. I was getting out of the car with the others when the officer in command said, 'Colonel Biddle, remain here; I will let you know when you are wanted.' I said, 'Major, you understand my word is pledged to go back unless everything is all right.' It seemed a long time to wait; I could hear them laughing and talking, apparently very jovial and having a good time. After a while I looked out of the door and saw one of Stoneman's officers coming. He looked very jolly and motioned to me very gaily. 'Hello, old man, what is it?' I said, and jumped out of the car. He held out his hand and said, 'Colonel, you are all right.'

"We all took a drink and looked at the rolls to compare them. We then took another drink and compared them again. Then we all talked over things and let the clerks, who also had had drinks, figure out the rolls to see how they compared. The Confederate officers who came down were fine fellows; after taking several more drinks and going carefully over the rolls it was found there were enough men to exchange for me, but on going back the officer in command said, 'Biddle, to tell the truth, I believe you were exchanged for a keg of whiskey,' and I found the bundle that I had noticed under the Major's arm was the small keg of whiskey. I immediately asked for the keg, as I wanted a correct picture of it to be introduced as a quartering on the Biddle Coat-of-Arms.''

NOTE.—Since writing these reminiscences, President Roosevelt has recognised the services of the Veterans of the Civil War, and has given each one, who had had no recognition, a grade higher than that in which he was retired, showing no favoritism, and also showing his estimate of our country's soldiers. It is safe to say that these men and their children's children will revere his memory, for there is no higher quality than gratitude.